THE PRIVATE LIFE OF THE QUEEN

HER MAJESTY THE QUEEN.
(*From a photograph by Messrs. W. & D. Downey.*)

The Private Life of the Queen

BY

ONE OF HER MAJESTY'S SERVANTS

With Illustrations

(FROM PHOTOGRAPHS BY MESSRS. W. & D. DOWNEY,
H. N. KING, AND HUGHES & MULLINS)

Gresham Books

in association with
Europa Publications Limited

First published 1897
This edition 1979

ISBN 0 905418 66 2

Gresham Books,
The Gresham Press,
Old Woking,
Surrey, England

Printed and bound in Great
Britain by Staples Printers Limited
at the Stanhope Press, Rochester, Kent

CONTENTS

		PAGE
PROLOGUE	. . . .	I

CHAP.		
I.	A PERSONAL INTRODUCTION . . .	4
II.	THE QUEEN'S PRIVATE SUITE AT WINDSOR.	11
III.	THE QUEEN AMONG CHILDREN . .	21
IV.	THE QUEEN'S KITCHEN	32
V.	THE QUEEN AS A HOSTESS . . .	38
VI.	THE QUEEN'S GUESTS	47
VII.	THE QUEEN'S RIDES AND DRIVES AND THE ROYAL STABLES	54
VIII.	THE QUEEN'S FADS AND FANCIES . .	64
IX.	THE QUEEN'S FORTUNE AND EXPENDITURE, HER CHARITIES AND GIFTS . . .	73
X.	THE QUEEN'S PASTIMES	82
XI.	THE QUEEN'S SERVANTS	92
XII.	THE QUEEN'S WALKS	101
XIII.	THE QUEEN AS A HOUSEKEEPER . .	108
XIV.	THE QUEEN AND HER STORE-ROOMS . .	115
XV.	WHAT THE QUEEN READS . . .	121
XVI.	THE QUEEN AS A DANCER	130

CONTENTS

CHAP.		PAGE
XVII.	WHAT THE QUEEN EATS AND DRINKS .	136
XVIII.	THE QUEEN'S PETS	145
XIX.	THE QUEEN'S RELIGION AND HER SUNDAY OBSERVANCE	153
XX.	THE QUEEN AS A WRITER	163
XXI.	THE COURT LIFE OF A MAID OF HONOUR	169
XXII.	THE QUEEN'S GOLD AND SILVER PLATE .	177
XXIII.	THE QUEEN AS A MUSICIAN AND ARTIST	186
XXIV.	THE QUEEN'S PRIVATE HOUSES (OSBORNE)	195
XXV.	THE QUEEN'S PRIVATE HOUSES (BALMORAL)	208
XXVI.	THE QUEEN AS A WORKER . . .	214
XXVII.	THE QUEEN'S GARDENS	225

LIST OF ILLUSTRATIONS

HER MAJESTY THE QUEEN . . . . *Frontispiece*

PAGE

THE QUEEN'S KITCHEN AT WINDSOR . . . 32

THE QUEEN'S BEDROOM 48

THE WATERLOO CHAMBER AT WINDSOR . . . 49

THE ROYAL NURSERIES 113

THE INDIAN ROOM AT OSBORNE 145

THE QUEEN'S DRAWING-ROOM AT OSBORNE . 193

THE EAST TERRACE AT WINDSOR 225

THE original book from which this edition is facsimiled was sent to me by an old friend who had kept it in the family Bible Box for many years. It is still neat and shining, and I experienced the thrill of opening a new and unknown book. The small dark red volume has a gilded title, and looking into it, I became absorbed in the minutiae of the Royal Household in the closing years of the reign of Queen Victoria.

Unfortunately for us, the writer chose, or was forced by circumstance to remain anonymous, and we only know this person by the pseudonym of "One of Her Majesty's Servants". In this context the word servant would denote a member of the Royal Household—someone very close to the Queen. The writer was perhaps disgruntled—certainly daring. There is one well-informed and detailed chapter about the Queen's Maids of Honour—could one of these ladies have written the book? However, in the Prologue, the writer describes herself as ". . . an humble Servitor to a Royal Mistress."

I assume the writer to be female advisedly, since most of the detail in the book could only have been observed so closely by a woman. However, we are given facts about the Queen's money; and although a woman at that time may have had access to accounts of the Royal finances, it would have taken a determined and well-informed character of either sex to write such a revealing chapter for publication in 1897. Whoever the author was, he or she showed remarkable tenacity in endeavouring to see that the book reached the reading public of Great Britain and America.

I have found evidence of five editions of the book, published in 1897, 1898, 1899 and 1901. Copies from the 1897 and 1901 publications are in the British Library.

My copy, from which this book is reprinted is one from the first edition of 1897. Its first owner was an unmarried lady of good family, who would have been in her mid-fifties at the time of publication. On the flyleaf of the book, in her own faded handwriting I have found the following words:—"This small volume is of some value because the unsold copies have been withdrawn—by Royal Command".

This little note gives us a clue to what is possibly the most intriguing aspect of the book. In England, in the last hundred years, it is unusual for any book that did not corrupt public morals, to be suppressed, and extraordinary that a book should be suppressed at the whim of the Monarch. Although the book may appear innocuous enough to us in the late 1970s, we can understand that the Queen would have been outraged at this unsolicited incursion into her private life. Obviously she had no prior knowledge of its writing, printing or publishing.

In 1897 the Queen was an old lady, enjoying the afterglow of her remarkable reign. It was also, of course, the year of her Diamond Jubilee, and no doubt she considered the publication of this book an act of impertinent betrayal by someone known to her, in the year when the British Empire was celebrating her sixty years on the throne.

C. Arthur Pearson Ltd. published the 1897 and 1901 editions, the latter being referred to as the "Memorial Edition". D. Appleton in the United States published the 1897, 1898 and 1899 versions, the authorship of the 1898 edition being ascribed to "A Person of the Royal Household".

The later editions appear to have been fairly successfully suppressed; I have found little evidence of their whereabouts in public libraries. However, some first edition copies slipped through the net to reach libraries, where a few survive to this day. Others would probably have been sent to favoured customers of the big bookshops—to those who had requested they be sent any new books about Royalty. Possibly the Queen herself as well as the original owner of this book received their copies in this way.

The 1901 "Memorial Edition" was apparently intended to run to 15,000 copies. This last attempt at publication, in the year of the Queen's death, with its consequent mourning, point once more to an opportunist and relentless author.

The Royal Library at Windsor Castle has a copy of the 1897 edition. It is significant that the book did not appear in the Royal Library until Queen Mary's time. The book contains a note saying that it was given to Queen Mary by a lady who told her that when it appeared the Queen was so angry that it was banned. Queen Mary added that the book must have been written by someone who knew details of the Queen's life intimately, and who knew much about her tastes and her rooms.

Researchers into the life and times of Queen Victoria have often used this book as a reference, and information from it has been woven into various works.

Although the origins of the book are mysterious and the path by which it has reached the reader devious, it contains facts to delight the amateur, and intrigue the professional historian. With this facsimile edition a much wider audience than ever before will have a chance to read this fascinating work.

EMILY SHEFFIELD

THE
PRIVATE LIFE OF THE QUEEN

PROLOGUE

M Y intention is merely to paint a family portrait of a dear old lady who, were she the *chatelaine* of a country house, or the schoolmistress of a primitive village, would be admired and beloved by her neighbours in the parish for her wisdom and good works, and by her family and servants as a good mother and mistress.

It would be easier, and to some more attractive, to paint an historical and heroic picture in bright colours, and so dazzle the eyes of the spectators with fine clothes, gorgeous heralds, and men in shining armour, that they would forget the importance of the central figure and the incompetency of the painter in the brilliancy of the surrounding subjects.

Though I may fail, it may be well to submit the outline sketch of my intent for your approval before I set about stippling in the lights and shadows, the details and colours which may, for all I can tell, destroy the likeness when they are filled in.

Briefly, then, my method is that of the old masters of

the Dutch school, as is best suited to a domestic subject. The central figure will be that of a sweet old lady, clad in homely, sober garments, as becomes a good housewife intent upon the affairs of her household, and I trust to portray by my modelling of features and by the gentle blending of pigments rather than by any lettering on the frame, the age, social position, sorrows, and joys into which she was born, as are the humblest of her servitors.

Following the method of masters of the Dutch school, the background will be somewhat realistic. The walls and furniture will faithfully reproduce the patterns familiar to her in her own private rooms, the pictures will be those which she has gathered round her as mementoes in her privacy of all she holds worthy in the past and present, and the accessories will be exact replicas of those of which she makes daily use.

As in a Dutch picture, the table will be spread, and upon it will be laid the plate and napkin she uses, the food and fruit of which she partakes, while the liquors she drinks will be faithfully displayed in the bottles and glasses which mark her tastes. In the bookcase will be the books she reads, in the fireplace the fuel she burns, on the floor the carpet upon which she treads, on the writing-table will lie her daily correspondence, and through the windows may be seen her favourite walks and drives, her horses and her dogs.

The method is not mine, and therefore needs no apology. Whatever the attainment, the object at least is a noble one, inspired by a desire born of sincere admiration, to in some way pay the tribute of an humble servitor to a Royal mistress. History, we know, is not best written by contemporaries ; but intimate personal details, if left unrecorded, are forgotten when they are most needed by the future historian, who would give his right hand to possess the lost sonnets of Michael Angelo, Dante's picture of Beatrice as an angel, the housekeeping book of Queen Anne, or the most foolish love letters of Queen Elizabeth.

There is another good reason why this book should be written while yet the subject of it is alive. Though even the most trifling detail that is here set forth is essentially correct, it stands to reason that there are others which, though not at present available, will be recalled and revived by the reading of these pages, and thus may lead to their being kindly sent to the writer for addition as footnotes to the volume. The most seemingly insignificant details will be acceptable, as they may throw a new light on the incidents and anecdotes which I have to relate.

I leave to others to depict the incidents in a reign as grand in war, as glorious in peace, and as golden in art, literature, and science, as that of either of Her Majesty's predecessors, Queen Elizabeth or Queen Anne.

My concern is merely with the petty personal details of the greatest woman of her time, who, when as a small child of twelve she first heard of her proximity to the throne, merely held out her little hand, and said, " I will be good!"

All political parties must agree that never was such a propitious promise more promptly given, or more royally kept by a young girl who became her own mistress at eighteen, and has lived through so many years of State anxieties and personal tribulations.

CHAPTER I

A PERSONAL INTRODUCTION

IF you stand in the Long Walk facing Windsor Castle and look to the extreme right you will see on the first floor of the Victoria Tower one large oriel window. That is the principal window of the Queen's private sitting-room. If you look a little farther to the right you will see on the same level a smaller window, which is that of Her Majesty's dressing-room.

If you stand at the extreme south corner of the East Terrace and face the Castle you will see two windows on the first floor of the Victoria Tower. The one on your left you will guess rightly to be the second window of the Queen's dressing-room. The one on the right, and a small window round the corner, facing due north, are those of Her Majesty's bedroom.

No amount of interest or bribery is ever likely to get you a nearer view of this suite. It is of all parts of the Castle the one sacred spot to which nothing but the Queen's personal " command " will gain you an entrance, and even then probably no farther than the private audience chamber, which is not one of the rooms that I have enumerated as being in the private occupation of Her Majesty.

But if you will follow me in the spirit I will try to give you some knowledge of the immediate surroundings of the Queen in her home at Windsor, which you may take to be typical of her other abodes.

At the far end of the quadrangle, in the south-eastern corner, the line of architecture is broken by the inner side of the Victoria Tower, which, from machicolated battlements to base, overhangs the side walk, and forms a portico beneath which the Sovereign, hidden even from the eyes of her own domestics, ascends to, or descends from, her carriage.

Up two shallow steps and through heavy oaken doors panelled in glass, lies the outer hall. It is small and octagonal in shape. The ribs of the Gothic roof are lightly touched with gold, but the prevailing tint is a creamy white. The inner doors, which are again of oak, lined with gold and pierced with glass panels, are flanked on either side by a fireplace set in deep embrasures. A huge grey marble vase, supported by bronze Cupids, and wreathed with flowers in lacquered bronze, stands on either mantelpiece. Three steps lead to the inner hall, from whence starts the Queen's private lift, a well-arranged apartment in oak, gold, and crimson upholstery. Beneath the light of an Empire lantern in ormolu and bevelled glass springs the staircase, which divides at the head of the first flight. Its white and gold balustrade of Gothic design, its crimson velvet hand-rail and soft pile carpet, lead straight to the Queen's private apartments.

To right and left of the large double doors, which give access to the Queen's private apartments, are two large pictures, the "Betrothal of Prince Henry of Prussia" and "The Jubilee Service at Westminster Abbey"; two excellent portraits of the Earl of Beaconsfield and the Marquis of Salisbury; and a statue of Edward VI. under a handsome Gothic canopy of white stone.

Before coming to all the treasures contained in Her Majesty's Sitting-room, Dressing-room, and Bedroom, it may be well in passing to look into her Private Audience Chamber, where she has received all the great men and women of the world, and the walls of which, if they have ears, have listened to many wise words and secrets more sacred than were ever uttered in the most closely tiled Masonic Lodge.

The apartment is not a very large one, though its slightly domed ceiling is lofty. The furniture and hangings are not very remarkable, though sufficiently rich and appropriate for a queen's reception-room. Yet the first glance round the chamber must convince the most ignorant that it contains within its four walls treasures that are almost priceless in their rarity and beauty. The double doors are of golden satinwood, inlaid with the finest marqueterie, and ornamented by large handles and finger-plates of beautifully worked gilt bronze. The wall space is horizontally divided into four, of which the lower division or dado is of the exquisite marqueterie, and the frieze or upper part is most elegantly and lightly decorated with the insignia and figure of St. George.

Directly beneath this graceful frieze hangs a line of masterpieces from the brush of Gainsborough, that for historical interest and rare artistic merit may well be deemed beyond all value. They are fifteen in number, and are portraits of George III., Queen Charlotte, and their numerous family of sons and daughters. Each portrays the head and bust of the Royal sitter, and each is set in an oval mount within a handsome square gold frame. No one in the world but the Queen can see in so small a space so complete and noble a collection of one generation of ancestors. For many years these fifteen Gainsboroughs held undisputed pictorial possession of the walls of Her

Majesty's Private Audience Chamber. But since the Queen has ceased to spend any appreciable portion of the year at Buckingham Palace, Winterhalter's charming studies of her nine children have been brought from there and hung under their powdered and patched forbears. These nine portraits are in circular frames, and show the little Princes and Princesses as really handsome children, with lovely complexions, and a profusion of beautiful, soft, curling hair.

Directly beneath these most interesting family portraits are a closely set line of glass-fronted cases, set panel-wise into the walls. They contain an extraordinary collection—miniatures, medals, enamels, medallions, and cameos—which is considered the finest of its kind in the world. Almost every face known to fame is to be found in this great collection of rarities, while every form of setting in jewels or chased metal work has been employed as surroundings for these treasures. This most extraordinary mural collection is crowned by two very massive glass-topped show tables, which stand on richly gilt legs on either side of the big double doors, and contain the very valuable collection of unset gems, historical relics, carved stones, and various curios known as the "Royal Gems."

The high mantelpiece, like all those in the Castle, is of the purest white marble, carved in a very airy design, and supported by noble figures in high relief. It is surmounted by a mirror and a sufficiently handsome clock and vases of marble and ormolu. At the right-hand corner of the mantelshelf stands a little thermometer in fine ivory, of a plain obelisk shape. Such a thermometer stands on the mantelpiece of every room in each of Her Majesty's residences. Except under the most baffling climatic conditions, these thermometers are never supposed to vary, and it is a most delightful characteristic of the Royal Palaces that rooms and staircases, halls and corridors, are always at an identical temperature.

If you are of middle age and your parents are alive, they may have told you that they once saw a slim and exceedingly pretty young girl in a black habit, accompanied by a number of ladies and gentlemen, cantering, under the green leaves in the springtime, along the tan ride of Birdcage Walk. Such a pretty picture of "an English girl on an English horse under an English tree," which was a great Frenchman's ideal, may have remained with you, and, therefore, you may be momentarily surprised as the door opens and a little old lady, to whom the art of becoming a grandmother has come gracefully, makes her appearance. It is a popular delusion, put into circulation by the Society Press, that the Queen has almost entirely lost the use of her legs.   This is very far from true ; but for some years— more especially since her accident—the Queen has chosen to facilitate her movements by the employment of a wheel chair in the passages and when suffering from acute rheumatism.   You must, therefore, be prepared to see Her Majesty enter either leaning on one side on a stick and with the other arm given to her Indian secretary, or slowly propelled into the room in an amply-cushioned wheel chair. In the latter case an Indian attendant, majestic and picturesque, will be standing behind her with the Lady-in-Waiting, and, perhaps, a Maid of Honour. If the Audience is likely to be of a business nature, the Private Secretary is in attendance.   If it is of a purely friendly nature, the Secretary and Indian attendant are dispensed with, and only the Lady-in-Waiting remains.

Those who expect great pomp and circumstance of attire at a Private Audience will be disappointed. The Queen is simply clad in a black stuff gown of easy fit and very unpretentious make, and her silver hair is smoothed away under a severely plain white cap, having small lappets at the back. As Her Majesty extends her hand to you to kiss, if you have an artist's eye and a sensitive touch, you will perceive that it is exquisitely white, soft, and dimpled, and perfectly moulded. In the plain gold circle and the memorial hair and gold rings which alone grace her fingers, you will read all the homely romance of a happy wife, a fond mother, and a sorrowful but resigned widowhood, which are the greatest attributes of a good woman.

There is a story told of a young and newly-appointed Equerry who, in going round the stables one day, came across a simple old lady in a mushroom hat and a countrified black gown. Filled with the importance of his new dignity, the zealous official shouted across the intervening stalls : " My good woman, you must get out of this ! Strangers are not allowed here, especially when Her Majesty is in residence." He finished up his remarks by threatening to take her to the gate himself if she were not quick in going. His feelings on discovering that the shabbily dressed intruder was his Royal mistress in person may be better imagined than described ; but the Queen, with delightful good-humour, forgave him and at the same time complimented him on his zeal and obedience to standing orders.

The story, which is true, is eminently characteristic of Her Majesty, for she carries her love of extreme simplicity almost too far. Among her immediate attendants she much dislikes being addressed as " Your Majesty," always insisting on the old-fashioned and homely " Ma'am."

If you are a student of photographs or portraits of the Queen, you will have great difficulty in recognising her in conversation. All I have ever seen are very far from doing her justice, for not only does she not photograph well, but her face in repose is very different from when she com-

mences to talk.   The kind, sad eyes light up, the nostrils
distend, the cheeks glow, the curves of the mouth turn up
in smiles and display a very pretty and complete set of
teeth in one so old, and the voice, instead of being husky
as might be expected, is singularly soft, and retains much
of that sweet singing quality which the great Lablache cultivated and Mendelssohn praised so highly in a private letter
to his mother.

The Queen is a singularly good talker.   Not only is she
well read in history, biography, and fiction, and speaks five
languages fluently—besides being a very fair Latin and
Hindustani scholar—but there is scarcely a picture or an
artist of any note in the world of whom and whose works
she is not intimately familiar, and she possesses an apprecia-
tive and practical acquaintance with the works of all the
great composers.   There is no music or musician too up-
to-date to inspire Her Majesty with the curiosity of a
student.   She is gifted with a marvellous memory, which
she has cultivated and preserved most carefully, not only
for faces and facts, but for all the little interesting characteristics which are the salt of good table talk.   Above all,
she is a sympathetic and eager listener, and so inspires a
person whom she desires to talk with encouragement, that
she quickly banishes all restraint and diffidence, and suc-
ceeds in drawing her visitor out into positive eloquence on
the subject in which she is interested, always herself showing just enough knowledge of the matter under discussion
to banish all idea that the listener is pretending to be
interested in a matter of which she only has a superficial
knowledge.   Besides this, she has a very pretty wit of her
own, and an enormous appreciation of any fun, being far
from *blasée*.   The Queen is the first to suggest and applaud
anything which would give pleasure in ordinary good society.

CHAPTER II

THE Queen's private apartments at Windsor are so intimately connected with her life, and are so characteristic of the passing events that have influenced her, that they lay a natural claim to a full description before her home-like rooms at Osborne, or her extremely simple surroundings at Balmoral.

From outside, the reader already knows the angle of the Castle that the Queen's private suite occupies. Approaching it from within, the first door opened is the massive portal of oak picked out with gold and panelled in the Gothic style, which prevails in so much of the restored woodwork at the Castle. It gives direct entrance to the Queen's sitting-room.

The Queen's sitting-room faces south. The first impression caught, on entering the room, is one of subdued richness and unostentatious comfort. The apartment is almost square in shape and of great height. It commands from the wide oriel window a fine view of the South Terrace, the Long Walk, the Home Park, and the Great Park. Nearly opposite the window is the mantelpiece, which is of white marble and of grand proportions. It is relieved with ormolu a casqued head being supported on either side by winged mythological figures and conventional wreaths. The reliefs to the uprights are Greek vases, supported by tripods, and surmounted by beautifully modelled eagles. The fender is a low one of brass wire, and the fire-irons are placed in small upright stands on either side of the grate, in which is burned nothing but beech logs; for though tons of coal are annually consumed in the Castle, the beautiful steel and ormolu grates of the State rooms and the private apartments never contain other than beech-wood fires, as the Queen has the same rooted objection to coals as to gas.

Above the mantelpiece is a mirror set in a cream and gold frame that matches the panelling of the room. The clock, of Empire shape, is flanked by a priceless pair of covered vases, two bronze military statuettes, and a couple of fine candelabra. Before the fireplace is a three-fold screen, and a long couch covered with luxurious cushions. Before this is placed a table over which is flung an embroidered table-cloth; it is generally littered with piles of photographs or laden with the illustrated catalogues of Royal possessions which are so extraordinary a feature of the Queen's household, and which merit a full description in another place. Directly behind the sofa stands an enormous round table, of beautiful inlay, which is, however, almost completely hidden by the fascinating confusion of books, photo-frames, and *bibelots* of all kinds, notable among which is a very charming equestrian statuette of the Queen, modelled when she was little more than a bride.

Recalling the stiff primness which characterised the apartments of the later Georgian era, and the singular degree of discomfort that marked the furniture and decorations of the thirties, it is strange to note the lavish crowding of pretty things, and the orderly confusion of beautiful *bric-à-brac* that make such a picturesque effect in the Queen's rooms.

Even the grand piano, a very handsome instrument, which stands beyond the round table, and close to one of the many doors, is not sacred from the crowd of *objets d'art* and dainty trifles that Her Majesty so loves to have about her. The high-backed comfortable chair before the keyboard is a comparative innovation, for the Queen is essentially conservative in details, and the princesses had much difficulty in deposing the uncomfortable "screw" music-stool from its time-honoured position. At the end of the piano, and tucked away in a convenient corner, stands the *étagère* containing the bound musical works which Her Majesty loves so well and which are in frequent request during the short time that elapses between Her Majesty's dinner and the hour for retiring. To right and left of the fireplace are two large cabinets which are crowded with china, statuettes, models of favourite animals, flowers, and photographs. Here I may remark that much as the Queen appreciates photographs, her most treasured mementoes of old friends and dumb pets always take the form of models. In clear Parian china, marble of all kinds, bronze, silver or gold, small busts, statuettes, and figures abound in profusion on all sides.

Well-stuffed couches surround the room at frequent intervals ; before them standing massive tables, each bearing its complement of books and portfolios.

Standing at an angle, so that the light from the window falls well across it, is Her Majesty's writing-table, surely the most sacred and the most interesting piece of furniture in the whole suite.

At the first glance it appears but a forest of framed photographs and miniatures of the Prince Consort and the Queen's family and friends. The blotter and writing-pad, the silver inkstand, fashioned like a boat, which four boys—two being winged and two being ordinary little mortals—are pushing across a rough beach; the chased gold pen-trays, the dainty cock's-head pen-wiper of solid gold, with a red cloth comb at the top of his head, and the quill pens which the Queen always uses, are not so easy to discover.

Before an array of framed familiar faces and writing materials stands Her Majesty's capacious writing-chair, with a narrow cushion across the back and a footstool beneath it, and on the floor at her right hand the dainty silk-lined waste-paper basket, the daily contents of which would be more interesting than a year's file of the *Times*. At the right-hand of the writing-table proper is a table in *étagères* of bamboo and lacquer, which holds the stationery-case, letter-baskets, and other paraphernalia necessary to an enormous correspondence. Another small table holds all the best published books of reference for the current year, which are uniformly bound in red morocco and stamped with her Majesty's cipher in gold.

Among the other occasional pieces of furniture is a small octagon table, which stands in front of the cabinet on the right of the fireplace, and has no other apparent use but to bear a tiny gold handbell, which summons Her Majesty's immediate attendants, while another is used by the Queen when in her rare moments of leisure she plays a game of "Patience."

The suite is entirely lit by huge chandeliers—wax candles alone being used by Her Majesty.

It is in the aspect of this small suite (for no one can fairly say that Great Britain's Queen and India's Empress is over-lodged in the four rooms dedicated to her personal use) that is to be found the keynote to the Queen's whole life. Here hang the pictures that recall memories, and friendships, or something even dearer. A pile of music lies here, an orderly litter of photographs and miniatures is

there, a small square book-stand holds half-a-dozen
volumes that are in course of being read, while everything
is dominated by bowls and baskets of flowers.

The Queen's private sitting-room might well belong to
any one of her wealthier subjects who possesses a simple
taste in furniture and decorations, a large collection of
pictures and sketches, and a full circle of relations and
friends. The general scheme of colour is crimson and
cream and gold. Heavy damask draperies frame the
windows, the lower panes of which are veiled with short
curtains of snowy muslin. The blinds are of a dainty
material called diaphene, in which is woven in a trans-
parent pattern the insignia and motto of the Garter. The
furniture is principally upholstered in the same flowered
crimson and gold damask that drapes the windows. The
walls are panelled in the same silk, and here, the constant
recurrence of the pattern (a conventional bouquet of
flowers) would become monotonous were it not for the
number of pictures of every description which cover the
walls from within a short distance of the ceiling of deep
cream and gold, to within four feet of the rich crimson
carpet, which is patterned with a delicate tracery of scrolls
and garlands in pale yellow. The many doors are painted
cream colour and decorated with floral panels and gold
mouldings.

This scheme of paint prevails throughout the suite, the
dressing and bedrooms only differing from the sitting-room
in that the walls of the former are panelled in a soft shade
of green silk, while the latter are papered with rich crimson
flock. The most striking features of the Queen's private
rooms are, to a casual observer, the pictures. In the eyes
of their owner each separate one has a history or recalls a
reminiscence. Chief among the portraits and landscapes,
the oils, water-colours, and crayons, are the many likenesses

of the Prince Consort. The best of these, which hangs in the sitting-room, opposite the fire-place, is a life-size, full-length picture, by Winterhalter, of the Prince, attired in black walking-costume and holding the top hat of modern times in his hand. But a most charming Landseer, that hangs above the cabinet on the left of the fireplace, also shows the Prince to great advantage. He is in shooting costume, and the fruits, in fur and feather, of his day's sport lie heaped at his feet. The baby Princess Royal, Eos, his favourite greyhound, and a Skye terrier are playing on the floor, while Her Majesty, in a plain gown of white satin, and with her slender girlish shoulders bare, stands at her husband's side. The picture, which was painted in the bay of the Green Drawing-room, has for the distant background a fine view of the East Terrace and the Park beyond, and is replete with grace and tenderness.

A delightful little picture in an old-fashioned gilt frame of carved wood shows the Prince Consort and the Duke Ernest of Saxe-Coburg, in velvet doublets, slashed with white satin, and wearing the collars and orders of St. George. Close by, hangs another portrait of Prince Albert in Stuart costume, the accompanying figure being a most dainty portrait of the Queen, dressed for the great fancy ball of Charles II. period, which was given at Buckingham Palace on June 13th, 1851. It is a singularly pretty likeness of the Queen. The Duke of Connaught appears twice in fancy dress, when quite a tiny boy of three. In one picture he wears the full panoply of an officer in the Scots Fusilier Guards; in another he is attired as bluff King Hal. Princess Helena (aged three) is represented in full Highland costume, and Prince Alfred, wearing his first middy's uniform. There is also a charming picture of Princess Beatrice, when ten months old. She wears a lovely white lace frock, and is lying on a white satin cushion.

In the Queen's bedroom hang two portraits of Prince Albert and his brother in their youth. Near them is a fine portrait of the Duchess of Kent, and also a pictorial recollection of her room, and the sofa on which she died at Frogmore in 1861, in the presence of the Queen, the Prince Consort, and Princess Alice. A sketch of the Queen garbed as a nun, standing with clasped hands in the presence of a vision of Prince Albert, is from the brush of the late Princess Alice. In the Wardrobe Room hang portraits of favourite gillies and pipers, among them being good likenesses of John Brown and Ross, Clark and Campbell.

Among other pictures to be found on the walls of the Queen's rooms are four different portraits of the Queen of the Belgians, in as many different costumes, and many likenesses of cousins and relatives too numerous to specify.

Two portraits of Baron Stockmar, most staunch of friends and sympathetic of advisers, are interesting. They show him as a kindly old gentleman with a shrewd face. A charming portrait of the Prince of Wales, when a child, is drawn by "The Queen and Sir Edwin Landseer." Other portraits, many of them being in tinted crayons, are Princess Mary of Cambridge (now the Duchess of Teck), a little girl all golden curls and ribbons ; the great Duke of Wellington ; a most quaint study of the Princess Royal when a baby, by the Prince Consort, and a lovely head of the handsome Marchioness of Douro.

Of sketches of Balmoral, Rosenau (Prince Albert's birthplace), Osborne, and the favourite apartments of the Queen at her different residences, there are many scores. It is perhaps worthy of remark that among the 231 pictures that adorn the Queen's private rooms, her daughters-in-law, her sons-in-law, and her grandchildren find no place, although photographs and miniatures of them abound on every side.

The mantelpieces and occasional tables in the Queen's dressing-room are as charmingly arranged and beflowered as those in the sitting-room. Here the green silk walls and hangings make a perfect background for the toilet accessories that cover the dressing-table. These are all of gold, worked and chased into most delicate designs. The mirror is set in a square-cornered frame that rises at the top into an oval. Before it lies a large gold tray, flanked by four scent-bottles of carved crystal. Two of these are set in gold filigree-stands of a shallow boat-shape. The pincushion is dark blue velvet, fitted within a gold-pierced edge. Of gold boxes there are about a dozen, and they are of every size and shape, ranging from the large square handkerchief box, to the small, nut-like patch-box. A pair of candlesticks, two large oval hair-brushes without handles, and a handbell complete the equipage. From the dressing-room floor rises some feet high, the magnificently elaborate gold stand which supports a lamp and "dressing-kettle" of the same precious metal.

The solid gold hand-basin, on the bottom of which are engraved the royal arms, has a romantic story attached to it. It was made especially for the Queen's use at her coronation, but after that event, "as strange things will, it vanished," and every effort to discover it completely failed. After twenty-seven years, however, when some structural alterations were being executed in St. James's Palace, a workman found, bricked in a hollow wall, the long-lost gold hand-basin. Since that time the Queen has always made a point of using it. As Her Majesty does not possess a golden ewer, a china one, that matches the rest of the wash-hand-stand fittings, is used. This fact may be worthy of the notice of friendly princes and privileged millionaires who are often at a loss to select a suitable and acceptable present to Her Majesty.

The Queen's bed is large and of wood, as are all of the beds at Windsor, the hangings being of fine crimson damask. It is most pathetic to note that above the right side of the bed there hangs against the rich silken background a portrait of the late Prince Consort, surmounted by a wreath of immortelles. The same sad memorials are in every bedroom that the Queen ever occupies.

The view from the windows of the Queen's bed and dressing-rooms is absolutely perfect, embracing as it does the incomparable East Terrace, with the tennis courts beyond, and in the distance Frogmore and the Great Park.

Perhaps the least noticeable, but quite the most charming and interesting sketch, is of a girl's small, white, dimpled hand, without the ring, evidently a Princess' hand, of which our greatest poet has said:

> " Princess-like it wears the ring
>   To fancy's eye, by which we know
> That here at length a master found
>   His match, a proud, lone soul its mate,
> As soaring genius sank to ground
>   And pencil could not emulate
> The beauty in this—how, how fine,
> To fear almost—of the limit line."

Who would think such waxen and such shapely and such sensitive fingers could sway the mightiest sceptre in the world for over half a century? It is a study of the Queen's hand, made when she was quite a girl, by Sir David Wilkie, for his picture of the Queen's first Council.

It is within the walls of these retired rooms that the Queen has sorrowed and joyed. Life and death have come to her, and power and patience have been granted her with which to rule her world-wide Empire.

CHAPTER III

THE QUEEN AMONG CHILDREN

THAT, during the regal solitude of her long life, the Queen should have devoted much of her time to, and the greater part of her love upon, children is not wonderful. They have been her dearest bond with her subjects and the one link that has bound her with all womankind, gentle and simple alike. The Queen has always had the true instinct of maternity very strongly developed, yet tempered with that discretion and common-sense, which with her have entered into the tenderest relations of life, and have never allowed her heart to get the better of her head. Born and brought up at a period when sentiment was cultivated as a fine art, she, even as a child, gave strong evidence of that independent spirit which later characterised two or three of her own children, and also of that generous frankness which she has always essayed to cultivate in all those belonging to her.

The following anecdote fully displays this early formation of the Queen's character : She was, when quite a little girl, taken on a visit to Wentworth Woodhouse, Earl Fitz-William's family seat in Yorkshire. Wet weather had made the paths in the grounds very slippery and unsafe, and the Princess, who was rambling ahead of the walking party, was warned of the fact by a kindly gardener, who in local parlance told her the paths were " very slape."

" Slape ! Slape ! What is ' slape ' ? " cried the Princess in the characteristically abrupt style that reminded those about her of the late King George III. The explanation which followed had no effect on the Princess " Drina," who started again on her wild career and promptly fell down in the mud. Lord FitzWilliam said : " Now your Royal Highness understands the word ' slape ' theoretically and practically."

" Yes," said the Princess as she picked herself up.   " I think I do, and I shall not forget it again."

Self-restraint was one of the first habits acquired by England's future Queen, who spent many months in every year visiting at great country houses, and it was also this carefully cultivated characteristic that made her endure with such courage what she has often described herself as her sad and lonely childhood.

Her doll's-house was her consolation in those days. It was a very homely affair compared to the luxurious palaces in which latter-day children keep their " babies." She was also childishly fond of making tea, and to this day her grandchildren and great-grandchildren can have no greater treat than to pour tea from a tiny melon-shaped silver tea-pot, with a very short spout and " May 24th, 1827," in-scribed thereon. The initial V, surmounted with a crown, which decorates either side, shows that even then her first name of Alexandrina was not used or favoured by all her family. This wee relic of the Queen's early days shows signs of much wear, for the butterfly poised on a rose, which makes the handle of the lid, has lost its outer wings, and they have never been replaced. A toy sugar-basin and teapot in silver, marked with a V and dated 1822, were also beloved by the Queen in her babyhood.

When her Majesty's own children began to arrive in the world, no trouble was spared from the birth of each to make it fit, physically and mentally, for the position to which it was born ; for, with all her deep love for her children, the Queen began at once to exercise the strictest discipline in her nurseries, and one of her oldest friends and most valued advisers always remarked : " *The* nursery gives me more trouble than the government of a kingdom would do."

This care was undoubtedly first rendered necessary by the fact that the little Princess Royal was at her birth a most sickly and delicate child, far different from the Prince of Wales, who was a fine boy from the first. It was at the dinner given in honour of the Princess' christening, that the vast gold punch bowl, which stands in the big dining-room at Windsor, and which was made for George IV. at the cost of £10,000, after designs by Flaxman, was filled with thirty dozen bottles of mulled claret.

Lady Lyttleton, who had been the Queen's governess, was early installed in the Royal nurseries, and superintended all arrangements for their proper supervision. To show how simple the baby Princess Royal, when only two years old, was, she was greatly pleased with two little frocks sent her as a Christmas present by her grandmother, the Duchess of Kent. All furniture and clothing provided for the children was exceedingly good and adequate, but wasteful extravagance and luxury were never seen in that department of the Queen's household ! All her children were laid in the same cradle which the Queen gave to the Duchess of York on the birth of Prince Edward. The christening robes, best lace veils and gowns, were all used by Her Majesty's babies in succession, while latter-day mothers should remember that Her Majesty always made time in her busy life to bathe with her own hands the last new baby. It was also with a view to always having her children under her own eye, that when the Queen's private apartments were being arranged by the Prince Consort for her at Windsor, the children's schoolroom was placed next to Her Majesty's private audience chamber, and one room away from her own sitting-room. This large and delightful apartment, which has views over the South Terrace, the stables, and the Home Park, is now used by Princess Beatrice. It is furnished with the greatest luxury nowadays, and rivals the Queen's rooms in the variety and quantity of its *bibelots* and photographs ; but on the walls still hang the numberless sketches and paintings executed by the Princesses of scenes in Scotland, pet animals and birds, and various essays at family portraits.

The birth of Princess Alice, in 1843, brought into the Royal circle the most charming and sweet of all the Queen's children. At first she was considered slow, although she was always admitted to be the beauty of the family. The Prince Consort often spoke of her as "poor dear little Alice," but she developed quickly, and soon became his favourite companion.

The Queen's method of education and upbringing was most excellent. One main principle on which she insisted strongly was that though their minds and bodies should be trained with regard to their future position, they should never be brought in intimate contact with Court life. Many of the Queen's ladies scarcely knew the Royal children save by sight, and by catching brief glimpses of them as they walked in the gardens with their parents or sometimes came into dessert after dinner. The most carefully selected governesses and professors taught the children English, French, German, and the Arts. Progress in their studies was reported perpetually to the Queen, who herself frequently supervised the riding and driving lessons which were given in the grand riding-school.

Generosity was inculcated, and on birthdays and at Christmas time the Royal children gave away with genuine delight, little gifts of their own making. Self-control was also largely insisted on, and when the little Princess Royal made her first long journey with her parents to Scotland, in 1844, the Queen herself was delighted with the self-possession of her little daughter in the face of salutes, guns, and cheering crowds.

Princess " Vicky," as she was called, also pleased her parents by her courage and sense on another occasion when in Scotland ; she sat on a wasps' nest and was very severely stung. The Queen was greatly alarmed on the occasion, but the child suffered the pain with considerable courage.

To encourage her children to speak foreign languages, the Queen frequently made them learn and act little theatrical pieces, while *tableaux* were another popular feature in the royal nursery. Also with a view to perfecting the Princes and Princesses in the more useful and domestic arts, on her birthday in 1854 the Queen made over to her children the lovely Swiss cottage and gardens in the grounds at Osborne, so that the boys should learn carpentering and gardening, and the girls the rudiments of cooking and housekeeping. Often the Queen would visit the cottage and be entertained there by her children. Most of her grandchildren have also used the pretty spot for picnic dinners and teas of their own providing.

The religious training of the Royal children was entirely mapped out by the Queen, who herself drew up a memorandum which, if it were given to the world in full, would prove of inestimable benefit to all parents, so kindly, so truly sympathetic, so earnest and womanly is it. Touching the Princess Royal in particular, she says, " I am *quite* clear that she should be taught to have great reverence for God and for religion, and that she should have the feeling of

devotion and love which our Heavenly Father encourages
His earthly children to have for Him, and not one of fear
and trembling."

The note touching the religious training of the Prince of
Wales was even more decided. " The law prescribes that
the belief of the Church of England shall be the faith of
the members of the Royal Family, and in this faith the
Prince of Wales *must unquestionably be trained.*"

But all this anxious thought on the part of the Queen
never degenerated into weak indulgence. Her sons had
almost more than their share of corporal punishment from
the hands of their father, and on one occasion the Queen
herself, for some act of disobedience, picked up the Prince
of Wales, and " reproved" him before the assembled
company. Being sent to bed in the daytime was the
chief punishment meted out to the Princesses, and the
Princess Royal, who, as she grew in years proved a very
high-spirited child, spent many more hours than she can
now count in the solitude of her own chamber. The
Princess Royal was, in fact, most difficult to manage. Her
wit and brilliancy of talent often led her to have a great
opinion of herself. She was yet but a tiny mite when,
being out driving one day with the Queen, she noticed,
and at once desired, some heather by the road-side. She
asked Lady Dunmore, who was in the carriage, to get her
some, but on being told that was not possible, as the
carriages were going too fast, cried : " Oh, I suppose you
can't, but *those girls* can get out and pick me some,"
pointing to the Maids of Honour.

The Queen's interest in children was never limited by
her own nursery. She always had kindly and tender
smiles for them all ; from those who attended at the yearly
children's balls at Buckingham Palace, or whom she en-
countered on her visits to her subjects' country houses, as

when she honoured her valued friend the Duke of Argyll at Inverary Castle, and first saw the Marquis of Lorne, whom she afterwards described as being "just two years old, a dear, white, fat little fellow with reddish hair, but very delicate features; a merry and independent little child," to the humbly born children of her servants whom she has so often handed to the minister for baptism, blessed with her own prayers and wishes, and ministered to as only a motherly woman can.

The Queen's delight and interest in the marriage of her sons and daughters was charming and touching in the extreme. Each fresh parting from the home circle was a grief that still was tinged with an anticipated pleasure, which was more than realised when the grandchildren began to appear on the stage of her life.

Like all the rest of her sex, the Queen is more indulgent to her grandchildren than she ever was to her own, and each young family in turn has been the object of her fondest care. For many years her interest in Princess Alice's children was proved every hour of every day, and her grief at the tragic death of little Prince Frederick of Hesse was as deep as the Princess' own. After the death of Princess Alice, the Queen made her beautiful daughters her special charge, having them often to stay with her, and providing them with *trousseaux* on their marriages.

The only grandchildren who have never been very sympathetic to the Queen, have been the families of the Prince of Wales and the Duke of Saxe-Coburg. Her Majesty is, however, deeply attached to her grandson's, the Duke of York's, babies, and often wonders whether little Prince Edward will turn out such a mischief-loving urchin as Prince George was in his youth. It was when the Prince was a lad, that his royal grandmother had occasion to reprove him for his want of manners at table one day.

As a punishment he was sent under the table when the sweets were being served. After an interval, pardon was asked and granted, and the culprit was ordered to come out. This he did—but in the same condition as Nature made him. The Queen was very angry at the time, but has since often related and laughed at the joke.

There is no doubt that the young ones now nearest to the Queen's heart are the children of the Duke of Connaught, and the babies of her own " Baby," as Princess Beatrice was called for many years in the home circle. These last-named little folks are all very beautiful children, and well merit the adoration bestowed on them. And how plainly that adoration is evinced is patent in every detail of the Queen's private life. At Windsor Castle, the rooms of the little Battenbergs are in the Victoria Tower, just above the Queen's own rooms, while her private apartments are never sacred from their childish raids, nor from the litter of a most miscellaneous collection of toys.

The humanity of Royalties can be gauged from their toys, for is not the child the father of the man ? Hence it is, that though every species of marvellous model and toy is lavished on the Queen's pet descendants, a very dirty rag doll or a wooden horse with damaged paint is a more frequent ornament of the Queen's private sitting-room than the beautiful organ which, at great cost, was made for little Prince Maurice a short time back. The Grand Corridor at Windsor generally contains a large hair-covered horse which is dragged up and down, and the beautiful surroundings of the pretty tea-house at Frogmore are happy playgrounds for Princess Henry's children. The verandah of the latter place is a fine storehouse for toys, and a big see-saw is just under the windows of the little tea-room.

At Osborne equal consideration is shown for the children, and they now occupy the same delightful suite of nurseries

that were so many years ago furnished by the Queen and
Prince Consort for their own offspring.   The splendid airy
rooms which command most lovely views across the Solent
and over the Osborne Gardens are in the Queen's own wing
of the house, and, as at Windsor Castle, have direct communication with her apartments.   As all nurseries should
be, the whole suite is arranged indiscriminately for sleeping
and living.   The largest of these rooms is almost the prettiest,
being decorated with a fresh white paper besprent with gay
flowers and bright chintzes that match.   A zig-zag patterned
carpet covers the floor, the entire centre of which is left free
of furniture.   A nursery-guard stands before the fire, and
two ample screens, one of scraps, the other chintz-covered,
mask the doors.   A round table, littered with toys, and some
side-tables bearing photographs and books, have their full
complement of wide, low chairs.   The cots in the room are
quite old-fashioned, being mahogany with cane sides, the
white fringes that hang round them forming an ideally neat
little valance.   The bedclothes have a simple arrangement
of strings, by which they are kept over restless little bodies
during the night.   Two tiny rush-seated armchairs suggest
delightful, childish days.   All round the room are literally
stacks of toys.   The pictures on the walls follow out the
Queen's taste in such matters.   A few are of sacred subjects, the rest are portraits, among them being likenesses of
the Prince Consort and of the children and their many
cousins.   Traces of the little ones at Osborne are found in
the shape of sundry toys in the Observatory Tower of the
house and down in Osborne Bay, where, in a well-arranged
floating bath, they learn to swim as their Royal aunts and
uncles did before them, as well as in the Lower Alcove, a
most delectable and picturesque garden retreat on the Lower
Terrace, which faces the big fountain and has a charming
view of the Valley Walk, where on wet summer afternoons

the Royal children have a picnic tea in just the same simple, homely fashion as the Queen so loved in earlier days.

Her Majesty's love and pride in her vast number of lineal descendants is pardonably great, and her curiosity to see the "newest baby" is always most delightful. That an early view may be gained by the Queen of the latest additions to the family, a small miniature likeness of the little stranger is always sent to her as soon as may be, which picture is worn by the Queen in a bracelet until such time as puts her reigning favourite's nose out of joint, when it is added to the large collection of these tiny pictures that the Queen possesses.

Although the Queen's private rooms at Windsor are filled with charming portraits of children, none, to my thinking, is so really beautiful in pose and execution as a picture I can recall of Princess Beatrice, painted when she was a year old. The beautiful baby, who is wearing an exquisite frock of fine, white lace, is lying at full length, and with dimpled, raised arms, on a huge white satin pillow, which billows up round the laughing child. As a picture of child-life, it is the gem of the Queen's collection.

Even the tiniest of the Queen's grandchildren is taught to treat his Sovereign with due respect. The smallest of them will doff his cap on entering the palace and bow before her, though the next minute he may be playing with the attendants.

There has been a great tendency to exaggerate to the public, the so-called interference of the Queen with the domestic affairs of her sons and daughters. That this is quite untrue is shown by the deep reverence and love in which all her family hold her. Even those more distant connections to whom she is a Queen first and a relation afterwards, hold her in the profoundest affection. On one occasion, a young English Prince, who is not very nearly allied to Her Majesty, visited Broadmoor, the great Criminal Lunatic Asylum. While there, he saw a wretched old woman, who, being informed of the identity of the visitor, at once burst forth into a frenzied torrent of abuse of the Queen. The Prince was horrified and most deeply moved, saying openly to those about him that his devotion to the Queen was so great that it pained him even to hear a lunatic rail against her.

One thing is certain, that if those who are grown up and perhaps getting on in years love and revere Her Majesty, the children who cross her path have every reason to adore her, whether they be of her own kin and can regard her as a fond and indulgent grandmother, or whether they be the offspring of those about the Court, her servants and her gillies, who, oblivious as children will be, of all rank, come nestling to her side, telling her their baby joys and griefs, and finding in her not only a queen, but a tender-hearted woman, who has been and always will be a true friend to little children.

CHAPTER IV

THE QUEEN'S KITCHEN

THE Queen's kitchen is quite the most imposing and unique department in the Castle. There is but one word to describe it fittingly. It is gigantic, and is the only place of the kind which reminds one at once of all one ever knew about giants, namely, Blunderbore's kitchen in a Drury Lane pantomime, where oxen are roasted whole and poor mortals are spitted like larks, so that the large gentleman with a club may have the pleasure of indulging his olfactory senses by sniffing the blood of an Englishman. Indeed, in these days of stage-realism, Her Majesty's kitchen might be produced in fac-simile at Christmas time, for, without either additions or exaggerations, it would provide ample opportunities for Mr. Charles Lauri and his accompanying sprites to run along mountainous ranges of dressers, and to hide behind enormous chopping-blocks or in cavernous ovens, when pursued by the giant and his large army of comic cooks.

The first effect that strikes the eye on entering is that made by some hundred brilliantly burnished coppers, each of different shape and all as big as a sponge bath. They are hung round the walls, and blaze like a million suns through a sulphurous London fog.

THE QUEEN'S KITCHEN AT WINDSOR.

The next object that claims admiration is the enormous "dishing-up" table, which is a good deal larger than the gardens of many suburban houses, and yet it is but an item in the centre of this vast apartment. Round it there is ample elbow-room for the army of white-capped and aproned men-cooks who bustle about, as also for six meat-chopping blocks, each as big as a good-sized dining-table.

But it may be more comprehensible to the mind's eye of my readers if I take this imposing structure in detail. As I have already hinted, it is as big as a barn, and as lofty. As you enter from either door you are faced by a large clock, which looks like a bull's-eye in the middle of a great wall. Immediately under this clock is the inscription :

"G. IV. Rex. 1828."

Immediately opposite, and facing the clock, is a fine head of a Royal stag of many points. Both these walls are divided by four immense close ranges—two on either side. These are each about twelve feet wide, and are marvels of convenience and completeness. It is in a long line above them that hang, like burnished shields, the Gargantuan coppers already referred to. Between these ranges are the dressers, wooden tables, and sinks, all being the acme of cleanliness and utility.

At either end of the room are the roasting ranges. They are somewhat old-fashioned, being quite open and of such huge size that six rows of large joints are cooked before each of them at the same time. The long spits are turned by chains, which in their turn are worked by a kind of chimney fan. Before each roasting-range stands a meat screen about ten feet high, and built into the wall on either side are enormous ovens. Surrounding the ranges there is a full complement of charcoal and gas-stoves, on which stand immense coppers.

It is in front of the fire, at the west end of the kitchen, that is roasted the great baron of beef which graces the royal sideboard on Christmas Day. At this same end of the room is an open fireplace that is diminutive in comparison with the others. It is used only for roasting the birds that go to the Queen's own table.

In due proportion to this spacious place is the lofty open roof, the floods of light from which are broken by the great oak beams that cross and re-cross beneath the skylight, and are reflected from the highly-glazed white tiles with which the walls are lined to the height of the potboard, which, with its accompanying coppers, forms an effective and uncommon frieze-rail.

The middle of the kitchen is, as I have before told you, occupied by the huge table of steel, which is polished to a state of extraordinary brilliancy. It is brass rimmed and stands upon brass legs, which are hollow. The legs and table are filled with steam which speedily heats the entire structure, on which are dished up the many large dinners of the Royal Family, the Household, the servants and retainers of the Castle, without the risk of the viands getting chilled in the somewhat elaborate process.

Many solid wooden tables, the six large chopping-blocks, and the desk at which the Clerk of the Kitchen keeps his accounts, complete the fittings of the spacious and smoothly sanded floor.

The Queen's kitchen is ruled over by a *chef* whose salary is close on £700 a year. For his convenience there is a small room set apart on the north side of the kitchen. It is a cosy apartment, furnished with a chest of drawers, washstand, table, and a most comfortable armchair. There is also a writing desk. Above the fireplace, which faces the window, hangs a china plate, mounted on a velvet plaque. It is emblazoned with the Royal arms, and was presented to the Queen some years ago by the Cook's Guild. The wide window-sill is piled up with blue paper-covered books, in which the Royal and Household menus are daily entered, along with the quantities of materials used in the different dishes.

Under the *chef* are four master-cooks who are on duty about a fortnight at a time. Add to these, two yeomen of the kitchen, two assistant cooks, two roasting cooks, about sixteen apprentices and a half a dozen kitchen maids, and the reader may imagine for himself the wonderful scene of orderly activity that prevails daily in this single room in the Castle, to say nothing of the scene when a State banquet is in progress.

Then it is that under the brilliant glare of numberless gas jets, the two great open fires roar up their wide-throated chimneys, while before the fierce blaze, two score of glistening, juicy joints, all crackle and splutter. White-clad cooks hover round monstrous coppers which fill the air with the hum of their bubbling. At his desk the storekeeper checks the quantities of food in course of cooking, or sends messengers flying to the storeroom for supplementary supplies. With the monotonous jangle of the endless chains that turn the spits, mingles the noisy stoking of the many different fires and the clang of the oven doors as they are sharply opened and shut. On the gas-stoves the *bains maries* hiss forth a most savoury steam of appetising sauces, while before their own particular blaze, fat chickens frizzle contentedly under the attentions of a roasting cook and his basting ladle.

Between one door and the great steel table (which is now glowing with a generous warmth) there is a constant stream of stalwart pantrymen bringing in the grand golden dishes, tureens, and sauce-boats, all of the same precious metal, which are in use to-night. Out at another door flock the footmen bearing the same dishes, so daintily dressed and served that they are indeed worthy "to place before a queen."

The entire scene, with its many mingled noises, the rush of feet, the hum of voices, the clatter of pots and pans, the ring of golden vessels, and the thousand different odours that rise in a cloud to the grained oak roof and hang in a heavy steam on the glass skylights, is like another edition of the *Walpürgisnacht*.

And yet only the heavier parts of a dinner are cooked amid these wonderful surroundings, for quite apart from it are the pastry-kitchen, the "green-room," where nothing but the vegetables are prepared, and the confectionery kitchen. This last is a most fascinating apartment, and the variety and beauty of the shapes and moulds to be found there, the charming little ovens and stoves which go almost all round the room, and the dainty appliances for "piping" and the more delicate parts of confectionery would delight any woman who is possessed of a "sweet tooth."

Within this confectionery kitchen is a beautifully-arranged room, all painted white, for the storing of the materials used by the confectioner and his half-dozen subordinates. Here also are packed the cakes and biscuits which, four or five times a week, follow her Majesty to Balmoral, Osborne, or wherever else she may be staying. Here, too, was made and packed the principal wedding cake of the Duke of York.

Before quitting this enchanting region of the culinary art, you will have noticed that all the walls are lined with white tiles, and that the scullery, which even in the best regulated families is a most unlovely place, is here a positive picture, with its spotless taps and sinks, exquisitely clean plate racks and tiled walls. It is characteristic of the extreme cleanliness that prevails in the Queen's kitchens, that all the floors are sanded, and that when necessary the sand is swept up and renewed half a dozen times a day.

CHAPTER V

THE QUEEN AS A HOSTESS

HOSPITALITY and the invitation of guests have been reduced to a fine art in the Royal palaces during the Queen's long reign. Certain curtailments have been made from time to time in the list of those who considered themselves eligible candidates for the Sovereign's entertainments, while on the other hand fresh additions are yearly made from the ranks of those who have merited the Queen's favour or excited her admiration.

To consider the present conduct of the State concerts and balls would be idle, as it is now very many years since the Queen has deputed to her daughters and daughters-in-law her duties as hostess on these purely formal occasions. Suffice it to say, that they are most splendid entertainments, at which every detail is in perfection of taste and lavishness. Yet a rider must be added to say that nowadays these functions lack the verve and interest which were once given to them by the charming presence of Her Majesty, who in former times moved so graciously among her guests, and, however great the number, made all feel personally welcome and at home.

At the balls which were given for the Royal children at Buckingham Palace, the Queen would lead every dance, and personally draw out the shyest of the little ones.

As a hostess on grand occasions and when she received the visits of crowned heads, Her Majesty's demeanour was at once stately and charming. Kings and emperors who went to Windsor were always greeted by her at the splendid State entrance, first with a deep reverence, then with a kiss, and the same procedure was observed at their departure. Only a few months back, when the Tsar of Russia visited his Royal grandmother by marriage at her simple country home in Scotland, the Queen greeted him with all the stately formality due to a sovereign, following her old custom of standing in the entrance at the head of her family and household.

State visits and State entertainments are, however, comparatively public property—they are conducted in the eyes of the world. It is rather with the quiet stream of visiting that goes on principally when the Court is at Windsor that we have to do, and the circumstances that surround these visits are very interesting, because they are quite private.

It must be premised that of the Queen's guests there are two kinds, those whose claim on her is one of friendship, in which case a visit of one to three days is expected, and those who for business, political, or other reasons, are placed on the "dine and sleep" list. In both cases, however, the surroundings and *locale* are the same.

At Windsor—which, as being the palace where the Queen now entertains the most, is best to take into consideration— the Visitor's Entrance is approached from beneath an ample porch in the north-east corner of the quadrangle, under the shadow of the Round Tower, and just past that quaint old remnant of Elizabethan days which now contains the Royal library. The entrance doors and those that divide the outer hall from the inner are of oak arranged after a good Gothic design, and set with panels of glass. The walls are of a creamy white, and, being ribbed and touched with gold, are very light in effect. The balustrade of the fine circular staircase is also white, with a hand-rail of red velvet, which matches all the carpets. A fine old eight-day clock on the left side, some oak furniture, a few pictures, and a well-executed bust in bronze of Alexander of Würtemberg, relieved with orders and ribbons of ormolu, all give an air of homely comfort and welcome.

On the right hand of the inner hall are the equerries' rooms, the one a library and writing-room, and the other their breakfast and lunch room. The first is a very plain apartment. A large round table fills the centre, and between the two windows, which are on a level with and overlook the quadrangle, is a writing-table.

Far more interesting is the breakfast-room, where guests usually linger on arrival and departure. Here the walls are of pale grey and gold, panelled in light oak mouldings. They are well covered by a most charming series of water-colour sketches, to the number of nearly fifty, representing the uniforms worn by the Household troops in 1832. There are also many pictures, the most attractive being a group of three portraits in one frame. A very pretty one of the Queen when a young girl, dressed in white and blue; Prince George of Cumberland, and Prince George of Cambridge. It bears the date 1832. The dwarf bookcases on either side of the fireplace are well stocked with reference and classical works, chief among them being such useful books as " Chambers' Encyclopædia," Knight's " Shakespeare," a " History of England," and the " United Service Journal."

Mounting the staircase, which is lit by handsomely chased brass oil lamps springing from the balustrade, the visitors, who are preceded by a member of the household, reach the vestibule, after passing beneath two pictures portraying Edward III. and the Black Prince, and a very beautiful stained glass window. A statue of King Alfred, the Jubilee picture of the Queen by Angeli, Caton Woodville's fine work, "Too Late," a portrait of Dean Stanley, and busts of George II. and Queen Caroline decorate this magnificent square landing.

From it, doors lead to that quaint white little room which inshrines forty-one pictures, including the most wonderful collection of Holbeins the world has ever known, a marvellous Cranach, and that historical old brass clock that passed as a wedding-gift between Henry VIII. and ill-fated Anne Boleyn on their marriage morning. It stands on a bracket of lacquered metal which is engraved with portraits of Henry and Anne, and has hanging from it disproportionately heavy weights. The Queen and her visitors pass through this beautiful little room on Sundays on the way to the Royal and Visitors' pews in the private chapel.

A small room in a tower just off the Holbein room (or Retiring Room as it is generally called) is only interesting for a round table it contains, made in alternate light and dark sections of oak and teak wood taken from the ill-fated *Royal George*.

It bears on a small silver plate in the shape of a ship the following inscription :—

Made of timbers recovered from the wreck of H.M.S. *Royal George*, sunk at Spithead, Aug. 29th, 1782. Presented to Her Most Gracious Majesty Queen Victoria by her most obedient and humble servants,

E. and E. EMMANUEL.

Portsmouth, Aug., 1841.

The small lobby which lies between the vestibule and the chapel contains a fine group by Wyatt, in white marble, of Penelope, bow in hand, and with a wolf at her side. Another door gives from the same starting point on to the Page's Waiting Room, a tiny chamber looking on to the quadrangle, which contains the life-size marble group of the Queen and the Prince Consort, in mediæval costume.

It was executed by W. Theed, in 1867. The attitude of the royal pair is touchingly affectionate. On the base is inscribed in gold letters: " Allured to brighter worlds and led the way." A large mirror is behind the sculpture. There are some good Zucarellis here, and several Canalettos. Also fine portraits by Angeli of Dean Stanley in 1877, the Hon. G. Wellesley, Dean of Windsor, in 1877, and of Sir Michael Biddulph in 1878. A very beautiful clock-case, depicting the Rape of Europa, is supported on either side by bronze figures of Oliver Goldsmith and Edmund Burke. This small room gives entrance to the Grand Corridor.

It is from this magnificent promenade that the more important suites of rooms are reached, and to show how well the Queen's guests are always lodged, we will consider the arrangements made for the three first ranks of her visitors: Crowned heads, her own sons, and her Ministers of State.

The rooms called the " Tapestry Suite " are always given to foreign Sovereigns, and so exclusively are they guarded from prying eyes that few who have not the right to occupy them have ever passed inside the splendid doors of oak and heavy gilding which inclose the apartment. The boudoir, which is the largest of the four rooms, is directly above George IV.'s gateway, and between the twin square towers of York and Lancaster. Those who know Windsor Castle from the outside will therefore remember that the large heavily-mullioned window of this room commands a grand view straight down the Long Walk to the Great Park beyond. Otherwise these rooms are very small, peculiar in shape, and not too well lit by daytime, owing to the windows being so deeply set. But they are given to the Queen's favoured guests, as they are very near to the private apartments of Her Majesty and Princess Beatrice, and quite close to the Oak Dining-room.

The tapestry in the suite consists of four very beautiful panels which were made at the Old Windsor Tapestry Works when they flourished under the patronage of the late Duke of Albany, as were also the very charming small panels which, set in borders of bright watercress green, serve to upholster the furniture. The tapestry gives rather a gloomy appearance to the room which is but slightly counteracted by the looking-glass, with which the inside of the doors is panelled, and by the gorgeous ceiling of cream and gold. The mantelpiece on the right is of grey marble, the shelf being covered with very valuable china, and some of the many hundreds of silver candlesticks the Queen possesses. Just opposite is a fine cabinet crowded with some priceless Dresden china and more silver *bibelots*. Close by the fire stands the piano, a full grand in a rosewood case. It was the prize piano at the Colonial Exhibition, and was made in Toronto, Canada. The Queen considers it is one of the finest instruments in her possession. Small tables full of books, china, flowers, and photos, are scattered about the room, which contains but two pictures, portraits of the late Emperor of Russia and the Dowager Empress, painted in their early married life.

A door cleverly cut in the tapestry leads into the first dressing-room, which is set in an angle of the Lancaster Tower, and is so dark that artificial light is almost always necessary there. Walls, ceilings, and doors are white and gold, and the huge maple wardrobe opposite the window is panelled with glass and decorated with gold lines. Some chairs and two fine satin-wood tables complete the furniture, but the pictures include many records of the Queen's family and ancestors. Queen Charlotte and Princess Caroline, by Lawrence, are delightful memories of those Royal ladies; a large water-colour by H. Thomas reproduces the gathering at Windsor Castle on the occasion of the christening of

Princess Victoria of Hesse, Princess Alice's daughter, in 1863. A very pretty little picture in an oval frame which faces the window shows the Emperor of Germany as a tiny boy in uniform. There are two excellent portraits of the late Emperor Frederick, one dated 1867, and a group of Prince Henry of Prussia and his wife. Likenesses of the first Emperor William and his Empress Augusta almost make complete this little gallery of the German Royal family, among which hangs a lovely picture of the Empress of Austria, painted at the height of her beauty. She is wearing a low white gown and her glorious hair is unbound and ripples far below her knees.

The bedroom is square. Six large cases full of miniatures decorate the white walls, and there are some delightful Georgian family portraits. The upholstery of the Amboyna wood bedstead and all the windows is of rich crimson silk damask. The wardrobe is of mahogany, lavishly gilt, but two small cabinets of Amboyna on either side of the fireplace are the prettiest things in the room. A second small dressing-room, in which a curtained recess is used for hanging dresses, contains a number of modern family portraits, and brings the suite to an end. It is these rooms that outside her private apartments are oftenest visited nowadays by the Queen, for here is always lodged her much-loved eldest daughter, the Dowager Empress of Germany.

In the York Tower are the apartments known as the Prince of Wales' rooms, but used by others of the Queen's children. The suite contains four rooms, numbered from 238 to 241. Portraits of the Queen's children at an early age, of the Duchess of Kent and the Queen as a very little thing, painted in 1821, the late Duchess of Cambridge, and the Dukes of Connaught and Albany, one in a Kharkee uniform, the other in a Scotch uniform, are on the sitting-room walls, which are covered in a rich-toned yellow silk. The piano is again of rosewood, and the furniture of fine Amboyna, relieved with chased ormolu mounts. Some very large mirrors give a bright air to the apartment. The most valuable piece of furniture it contains is a lacquered Japanese commode with a white marble top.

The bathroom in this suite is strictly utilitarian. The bedroom has a gold ground paper. The well-known picture of the Queen at the age of three hangs here, also a charming portrait of her on horseback and wearing the flowing habit of 1839. The hapless Princess Charlotte is also portrayed. The furniture is of mahogany and Amboyna. Everything makes for intense comfort without any great display.

Just under the Tapestry Suite in the Lancaster Tower, and numbered 343, are the rooms that long custom has dedicated to the use of the principal Ministers whose visits to Windsor during the session are very frequent. The suite, which is entered by a door at the foot of the tower, is most comfortable, and comprises two bedrooms and a sitting-room, arranged with everything necessary for the despatch of business. Bright flowery papers cover the walls, and the furniture everywhere is upholstered in chintz. The sitting-room contains eight good pictures of the Dutch school, a medallion portrait of Lord Beaconsfield, a portrait by Sir Joshua Reynolds, of Edward, Duke of York, a picture of " The Landing of the Elector Frederick at Gravesend," and a well-filled and very handsomely carved bookcase.

The bedrooms are pictorially decorated with portraits of the Countess of Essex and of Alphonse D'Avalon and his mistress, after Titian.

The accommodation for visitors at Osborne is much better than it used to be, as, when the Indian room was built there, a large number of excellent bedrooms were arranged above it.

At Balmoral it must be confessed that the arrangement for guests outside the royal circle is very indifferent, and the Minister-in-Attendance is obliged when there to transact all his work in his bedroom. This lack of space was, however, designed on the part of the Queen and Prince Consort, who always tried to make Balmoral as much of a holiday resort as such busy people are ever able to enjoy.

And now that the guests are in their apartments dressing for the nine o'clock dinner, we will leave them, and pass on without hesitation to the consideration of the Grand Corridor where every one awaits the Queen, and of the Green and White Drawing-rooms, which, with the Crimson Drawing-room, make up the private reception-rooms so frequently used by Her Majesty. Thence to the equerries' billiard-room, and the unaffected and friendly way in which the Queen entertains her guests after dinner is over.

With regard to those who are " commanded " to Windsor for a short interview with the Queen, the visitor is generally taken to the beautiful Audience Chamber in the Sovereign's private suite. A maid of honour first receives the guest, and then the Queen enters with a lady-in-waiting, an Indian servant, and perhaps a secretary, according to the nature of the audience.

Very often one of the Princesses accompanies the Queen. After the interview the guest is generally invited to luncheon with the household.

CHAPTER VI

THE QUEEN'S GUESTS

IT is in the Grand Corridor and in the vicinity of Her Majesty's private apartments that the guests and Household assemble between half-past eight and a quarter to nine o'clock, and there await among regal surroundings the arrival of the Sovereign and the signal for dinner.

The *coup d'œil* of the Grand Corridor is the most striking sight in the whole Castle, and the treasures it contains only serve to enhance the richness of the crimson silk draperies which are hung from elaborately gilt cornice-poles, the wonderfully bossed and gilded cream ceiling, and the exquisite contrast of the many recesses fitted with oak and gilt boxes, which are always filled with foliage and flowering plants. The floor is of inlaid woods, and the walls, being a pale, soft grey, form a perfect background for the interesting collection of pictures, and for the large lamps that on carved and chased gilt standards everywhere raise their glowing heads.

Between the arches of oak and gold that break the straight lines of the corridor, and opposite the long line of windows that overlook the Quadrangle, stand at intervals a wonderful assortment of cabinets, some of the finest Boule work and others of Japanese lacquer, but all alike lined

with white satin and having shelves of plate-glass. In them
are set forth many specimens of Sèvres, notably some pieces
of *vert pomme* and blue *œil de Perdrix*, the three famous
Rose du Barry vases, which are without rival in the world,
some very extraordinary mauve Chelsea vases with different
fruits as handles to the covers, and a great deal of remark-
ably fine Dresden. In fact, the china contained in the
Corridor at Windsor is considered beyond all price and, in
the mass, quite unpurchasable.

The many pictures, beginning with " The Queen's First
Council," by Sir David Wilkie, which illustrate so well the
various important events of Her Majesty's reign, are too
 ntimately known to the public through the medium of
engravings to need any description here. They number
more than twenty and are distinctly interesting, although
by no means the highest forms of art. A picture, however,
that is really touching is entitled "The First of May, 1851,"
and represents the aged Iron Duke of Wellington presenting
a golden casket to his royal godson, the baby Prince Arthur,
who lies in the Queen's arms, while the Prince Consort leans
over Her Majesty's shoulder.

Several lovely Gainsboroughs, a Reynolds representing
Princess Sophia Matilda playing on the ground with a Skye
terrier, Hogarth's fine portrait of Garrick and his wife, two
or three of Zoffani's quaint interiors of famous picture
galleries, and several good examples of Canaletto's peculiar
style, leaven the more modern paintings. Two models of
Ancient Rome in marble and ormolu stand near a very
sweet bust of the Queen, taken when she was ten. An
excellent likeness also must have been Chantrey's bust of
her in 1839. The most singular pieces of sculpture in the
whole Corridor are, however, two seventeenth century busts
of heroic size of Roman Emperors. They are in red
porphyry and oriental alabaster, and are very ugly, though

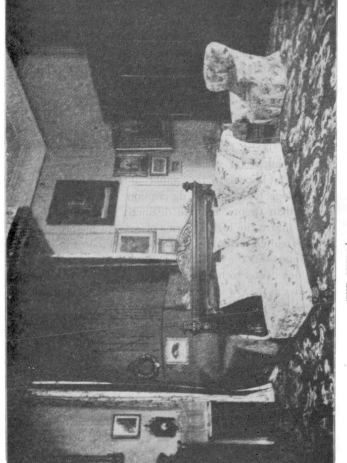

THE QUEEN'S BEDROOM.

THE WATERLOO CHAMBER AT WINDSOR.

(*Used as Her Majesty's private theatre.*)

not without interest. Four pedestals, hewn from the rock at Gibraltar, are curious. The bronzes, which are on all sides, are beautiful, several of them being most gracefully modelled. A group in silver and gold of " Lady Godiva " was given by the Queen to Prince Albert, August 26, 1857. Another grand piece of plate always standing in the Corridor is the great silver vase presented to the Queen at her Jubilee by the members of the Household.

A point of everlasting speculation with the public is the identity of the *real* resting-place of the Koh-i-noor. It may interest many, therefore, to know that it is kept in the Grand Corridor at Windsor.

But more than the big diamond, the silver and the gold and the rare china, does Her Majesty prize the plain Bible, bound in limp leather, and with overlapping edges, that belonged to her faithful servant, General Gordon, and was brought to her by his sister some time after his sad death. The simply bound book is inshrined in a seventeenth century fairy-like casket of carved crystal, with silver-gilt and enamelled mounts. It lies on a cushion of white satin, and is open at the first chapter of the Gospel according to St. John, pp. 64 and 65, which are marked in blue pencil. The Queen likes all her visitors to see this relic of a great man's life, and on more than one occasion has herself directed attention to it, and always with words of great feeling.

Should Her Majesty desire to retire early to her own rooms, the company return after dinner to the Corridor, where they stand until their Royal hostess has addressed each one in her kindly and thoughtful fashion, always remembering the tastes or circumstances of everybody, and never omitting to inquire by name after those of a family whom she knows. This is one of the minor courtesies of life about which the Queen is intensely punctilious.

After the withdrawal of Her Majesty, the guests are free to adjourn to the Crimson Drawing-room, which will be described as being the scene of so many of the merry small dances the Queen was once so addicted to giving.

Should, however, any music be arranged for the evening, or should any gifted amateurs be staying at Windsor, the Queen leads the way to either the Green or White Drawing-rooms, apartments she now prefers to the Crimson Drawing-room, which is almost exclusively used by the Household.

The Green Drawing-room is extremely startling at first sight, for the richly flowered silk which covers both furniture and walls is of the most brilliant apple-green hue. A second glance, however, convinces the visitor that the colour is at once the most delightful and most becoming that was ever used in decoration. The apartment is large, well proportioned, and broken by a very deep bay with a large window at the end overlooking the incomparable East Terrace. It was in this bay that Landseer painted his loveliest picture of the young Queen, in company with the Prince Consort and the baby Princess Royal, who sports on the floor with some dogs. The picture hangs in the Queen's private sitting-room, and is an ideal portrayal of happy family life.

The famous Sèvres service of fine *Bleu de Roi* made for Louis XVI., and bought by George IV. for £40,000, is in this room, as well as the four candelabras of bronze and ormolu representing the "Four Seasons," which date from the early period of Louis XV. Many other bronzes, a splendid black Boule table and inkstand, and two portraits by Lawrence, on either side of the fireplace, are chief among the art treasures of this most beautiful room.

Her Majesty's favourite apartment is undoubtedly the White Drawing-room. Smaller than the other two, its walls and ceilings are a vision of white and gold, while the gilt furniture is upholstered in royal crimson and gold silk. The most remarkable features about this dainty spot are two large doors in polished ebony on either side of a huge mirror. They are heavily decorated with ornaments in ormolu, and lead to the private rooms of the Queen and those which were used by the Prince Consort respectively.

Carefully guarded by glass screens is the lovely Gouthière cabinet, famous as containing the finest panels that the Sèvres porcelain works ever produced, and the best work in ormolu that the great craftsman Gouthière ever executed. It dates, as does a second one, from Louis XVI.'s period, and experts have valued the pair at an immense sum. Two very pretty portraits of George III.'s daughters, the Princesses Mary and Sophia, are by Hoppner, and a picture of Queen Charlotte in her young days, by Cotes, is eminently pleasing. One of the many Winterhalter portraits of the Queen, painted in 1842, hangs here. He was always considered by the Royal family to be the only artist who ever rightly caught the expression of Her Majesty's mouth. A sweet picture shows the Prince of Wales at a very early age, wearing a white satin frock and a profusion of curls.

In the window is an enormous vase of gilt china, sent by the Emperor Nicholas of Russia to the Queen in 1844. In panels it bears pictures of Peterhof and the Marble Gateway of the Winter Palace.

In all these drawing-rooms there are large candelabras on tall standards, handsome chandeliers, and exquisitely carved mantelpieces of white marble, while the double doors that connect the suite are all heavily ornamented with chased ormolu wreaths and festoons. Candles form the illuminant power, as Her Majesty has a great dislike to the heat of gas and the glare of electric light. In all the fireplaces here, as in the Queen's private apartments, nothing but beech-logs is burned.

The elegant White Drawing-room has for some years past been the scene of all Investitures held at Windsor, and when last Eleanor Duse, the Italian actress, was in London, she played *La Locandiera* before Her Majesty in this room.

Should professional music be the order of the evening, a short set programme, which has previously been submitted to the Queen, is gone through, and the dinner party is augmented by a few of the Household, and of the Queen's friends from the immediate neighbourhood. If amateur talent is relied upon, the Queen indicates in turn those whom she would like to hear sing or play, and on these occasions those of the Princesses who are at the Castle always assist in the evening's amusement. It was on such an evening that Her Majesty asked one of the maids of honour who had been—according to Court etiquette—standing for some time, to sing a song. The young lady begged to be excused, saying she had a bad cold.

"Then you had better go to bed," said the Queen.

"No, thank you, Ma'am, but I should like to sit down!" answered the lady.

Sometimes music is abandoned in favour of chess or cards, both of which pastimes in connection with the Queen's private life will be considered later. But however the evenings may be spent, they are always most pleasant. The ladies, in turn, approach, and are generally invited to sit by the Queen's side ; the gentlemen are free to stand and move about as they please. It is the rule, however, not to raise the voice when speaking, and loud laughter is considered a gross breach of courtly manners.

The Queen leaves her guests betimes, going to her own rooms to read and transact business. Every one curtsies and bows as Her Majesty departs. Should she desire later in the evening to have an interview with any particular person, he or she is sent for to her private suite.

After the Queen's departure the party quickly breaks up, the ladies going to their own rooms and the gentlemen downstairs, to the equerries' billiard-room, which, by the way, is used by visitors of every degree, as there is no other in the Castle. A turn in the corridor that leads from the visitors' entrance gives immediately into the ante-room, a small place containing two very quaint pictures. One is a portrait of "Mr. Theodore Panden, Keeper of Her Majesty's Royal Palace, in Windsor Castle, in ye reigns of Charles II. and King James and King William, Sept. xiii., MDCC., also to Queen Anne and to King George."

The other represents an old woman in an apron, and with a broom in her hand. It bears the date 1686, and the name of Bridget Holmes.

The billiard-room itself is commonplace. A grey-blue paper covers the walls, and the table is lit by six oil lamps.

It forms a strange contrast to the splendid billiard-room at Osborne, which is one of the noblest apartments in the house, but, on the other hand, is perhaps more comfortable than the same apartment at Balmoral.

Although the Queen seldom, if ever, sends for any of her guests before they leave next morning, every provision is made for their amusement. On a first visit most people express a desire to examine the treasures of the Grand Corridor or to inspect the library.

In fine weather they stroll in those parts of the garden the Queen is not likely to pass in her morning drive, while those who are interested in fat stock and such-like walk to the Shaw Farm.

Between eleven and twelve o'clock all "dine and sleep" guests have left the Castle, after a visit which even to the most *blasé* must be a memorable and delightful experience.

CHAPTER VII

THE QUEEN'S RIDES AND DRIVES AND THE ROYAL
STABLES

IN the early twenties it was quite the fashion among smart people, or those humbler folk who had come from the country a-sight-seeing, to walk to Kensington Gardens, there to see a little girl in a low chaise being drawn by a fat pony under the shade of the fine old elms. That little girl was our Queen, who could both ride and drive when she was six years old, and who since then has never lost her taste for carriage exercise nor her appreciation for good horseflesh.

In her early married life the Queen rode a great deal. She had a charming seat and any amount of courage. King Wilhelm of Prussia admired her on horseback immensely, and after his visit to this country to attend the Prince of Wales' christening, he sent her a magnificent animal called " Hamo," which she rode for seventeen years, and a model of whose head is now placed above the entrance of the great riding-school at Windsor, where all the Queen's children and grandchildren have learned to ride, and where on one occasion Sanger's Circus gave a performance before Her Majesty.

In Scotland the Queen for many years almost lived on

pony-back, and her memories of " Flora " and " Jessie,"
who carried her so long and so safely, are very kindly and
womanly. Indeed it is only within the last year that the
Queen has really ceased to ride, for it has, until quite
recently, been her habit to mount a sure-footed pony when
making expeditions in places too steep or narrow for her
chair to pass.

Almost the first thing the Queen and Prince Albert did
after they were thoroughly settled down at Windsor Castle
was to rebuild the stables. These fine buildings, which lie
on the south side of the Castle, form another tribute to the
wise perception of the Prince Consort, while the entwined
V.A., which is placed upon every wing of the many struc-
tures, are but added proofs — if such are needed—of the
complete accord which existed between the royal pair.

All the royal stables are arranged in a series of the most
airy and roomy loose boxes, not more than about a dozen
forming what is called a " court." Prince Albert never
believed in crowding a number of animals under one roof.
The most famous stable at Windsor, and that which was
ever the favourite of the Queen, is " Grey Pony Court."
Her Majesty used at one time to visit the " Court " each
day, and knew every horse kept there. These splendid
animals, although called ponies, are really very fine horses
being about seventeen hands high. At one time nothing
but greys ever had the honour of drawing Her Majesty, but
now she uses a good pair of bays with black points. The
innovation of a pair of strawberry roans, which were purchased about four years ago and broken for the Queen's
use, resulted in an accident and a return to the steadier
greys and bays.

In these days about eighty horses generally stand in the
Castle stables when the Court is at Windsor, but there is
room for more, while many of those there are not available

for general use. When extra horses are required they are jobbed from accredited people in Windsor. Among the non-usable occupants of the splendid boxes are four Arab stallions, one being white, and a Jubilee present. No one ever rides these except one of the Queen's Indian servants, who often pleases his Royal mistress by giving an exhibition of feats of skill on one of these almost wild creatures.

The donkey "Jacko," who was bought out of pity by the Queen at Nice one year, and who is now fat and sleek, and is used both for Her Majesty's garden chair and as a steed by Princess Henry of Battenberg's children, is another uncommon visitant in a stable. The little Princes also have a pony called "Prince." The horse that their father, the late Prince Henry, used as a hunter is a magnificent black bay, of great height and strength. Princess Henry owns, and frequently drives as pairs or as a team, two beautiful blacks and two bays. They are named, "Gloaming," "Midnight," "Noon," and "Dawn." The Princess' favourite ponies were bred at Hampton Court, and are named "Tarff" and "Wave."

The riding-horses used by the Maids of Honour and the Equerries are all bays, and like all the Queen's horses, are large, upstanding animals, for not unfrequently are they, perforce, put to other purposes than merely trotting under a light weight.

The harness-rooms at Windsor contain much that is interesting. A dainty arrangement in brass and leather, with two big fox's brushes hanging over the blinkers and sundry bells, forms "Jacko's" holiday attire. It was made for him on the Riviera at the time the Queen purchased him.

The most curious harness is kept very carefully under glass. It is called "The Quill Harness," as the entire leather work is patterned over with a most delicate lace-like design, wrought out in white quills. It was made soon after her marriage for the Queen's four favourite greys, but a misunderstanding arose about the contract for it, and a law suit ensued. The Queen won the case ; but, by Prince Albert's desire, the harness was never used. The ordinary harness which is used at Windsor, or at any of the Queen's country houses, is heavy and plain in make. It is very strong, as the Royal carriages are of great weight.

But to see all the Queen's horses and carriages in the glamour of imposing state one must visit the Royal Mews at Buckingham Palace, where are lodged the exquisite coaches and carriages and the valuable horses that Her Majesty regards with pardonable pride.

Though scarcely an imposing or beautiful block of build-ings, the stables attached to Buckingham Palace are most suitable for their purpose. They were originally planned and built by George IV., but were entirely remodelled by the Prince Consort on the lines laid down by him at Windsor. They are built round a large quadrangle, one side of which is open to the Palace grounds, and they are easily overlooked from a little summer-house of rustic design, where till a few years ago Her Majesty frequently took tea on a fine afternoon.

About 120 horses are generally kept in the stables, though when visitors are staying at the palace, in the height of the London season, the number is sometimes augmented with horses from Windsor or from certain job masters. Besides the Royal family, visitors and their households, the Master of the Horse has the run of the Royal stables, and may use freely anything therein, except the cream ponies, the State blacks, and the State carriages. It is among the duties of the head coachman at Buckingham Palace to call daily for orders at the private residence of the Master of

the Horse, who, however, in these days, has practically no
jurisdiction over the stables at Windsor.

Among the many score of fine horses which form the
glory of the Queen's stables are the celebrated cream ponies
— like the greys, some seventeen hands high.   These
wonderful Hanoverian horses were first brought to England
by George I., who used them on all State occasions.   When
the Queen came to the throne, however, the Royal stables
were innocent of cream ponies, and the King of Hanover
sent Her Majesty eight of them as a present.   The breed
has for some time now been extinct in Hanover, and those
the Queen possesses were all bred at her stud farm at
Hampton Court.   They are handsome animals, of a heavy
build, all entire horses, and with long manes and tails of a
deep cream colour.   Like all thoroughbreds, they are never
clipped.   Their strength is very great, and is necessary for
the weight of the celebrated red morocco harness used on
grand occasions.   This harness, each set of which weighs
one hundred and forty pounds, was made for William IV.,
but was never used in his lifetime.   The morocco trappings
are entirely overlaid with finely-chased and gilt metal work.
There are no collars, but the saddles for the postillions are
of considerable size and weight.

Next in value and interest to the cream ponies are the
blacks, a very beautiful team of horses, which are used by
the Prince and Princess of Wales for Drawing Rooms, and
by the Queen for semi-State ceremonials.   The harness
brought out for these striking and very valuable creatures
is of black leather with ormolu mounts, red saddle-cloths
and rosettes.   Neither these blacks nor the creams are ever
taken abroad by the Queen.   They are all too fine a breed
to be subjected to the risks of travelling and strange
stabling.   The creams in particular are very nervous
animals, and exceedingly delicate and restive.

All the horses in the Queen's stables, whether her own property or merely jobbed by the month, have to undergo a special training before they are considered safe for the use of any members of the Royal family or their suites. After they have been duly broken to harness, they are driven day after day past every kind of military band. They are taught to bear with perfect equanimity the beat of drums and the scream of fifes, the blare of trumpets and the skirl of bagpipes. Then they are made to stand by railway trains and to hear every sort of whistle and roar and rattle. Before any great public ceremonial the horses to be used in the procession are walked through a howling and applauding crowd of grooms, helpers, and stable lads. Finally the horses have to be broken to firing. This is done by taking them down to Aldershot on a field day, and at one time, when Her Majesty was in the habit of frequently attending reviews, this method was perpetually pursued.

Apart, however, from the world-famous creams and blacks, the Queen's stables in London contain some of the finest horses in the world, and until recent years Her Majesty invariably went to see her equine pets during her visits to town. Even now she frequently goes through the Royal stables in her little pony-chair.

At Buckingham Palace, as well as at Windsor, Osborne, and Balmoral, the plainness and neatness of the stable fittings is remarkable. The name of every horse is inscribed on a blue scroll above its manger, but the brilliant colouring, expensive tile work and nickel ornaments that distinguish so many "smart" stables are absent. The floors of all the harness rooms are sanded, a most clean and sanitary plan.

It is a noteworthy fact that no horses that have ever been in Her Majesty's service are killed when old age renders them unfit for work. They are either drafted to the royal farms, or more generally are put out to grass. Also, the Queen prides herself on the fact that no horse in her stables has ever been docked. Her Majesty has a horror of the practice, and considers it both unnatural and cruel.

Although until very recent years the Queen has been physically an extremely active woman, and has done, by her own showing in her diaries and letters, an enormous amount of walking and riding, it has followed, as a natural consequence of her high state, that driving has played a very important part in her life. From the time when, as a little girl, she drove her simple pony carriage about the quiet Kensington streets or still more retired lanes of Devonshire, Her Majesty has been accustomed to driving. After her marriage the vehicle was sometimes changed, for one very hard winter she spent many hours in sleighing at Brighton with the Prince Consort and baby Princess Royal, during the only visit she ever paid to that town.

Most of the attempts on Her Majesty's life were made either when she was driving or leaving her carriage, and it was this which for many years caused her to drive at such great speed.

This practice proved most fatiguing to those who ever accompanied the Sovereign, and on one occasion, when he was well set in years, the Duke of Wellington became so exhausted while riding at the Queen's wheel, that he was forced to return to Windsor Castle, to his great chagrin. The Queen now, however, does not drive fast unless time has been lost on the road. Her Majesty is most punctual, and never gives her coachman more than five minutes' grace. But the Queen can no longer lay claim, as she once could, to possessing the fleetest horses in England.

Yet, if Her Majesty's horses have changed of late years, the same cannot with truth be said of her carriages, the interesting and varied collection which fills the spacious and lofty coachhouses forming an important part of the magnificent stables at Buckingham Palace. Many of the carriages there are a quarter of a century old, and there are at least a dozen of them which are connected with the most important and historical events of Her Majesty's long reign.

First and foremost amid this array of eighty-eight conveyances is the State Coach. This is not only valuable on account of its intrinsic worth, but also because of the historical associations interwoven with its own period of existence. Originally built for, and first used at the coronation of George III., George IV., William IV., and Queen Victoria have all driven in it to their coronations. It was also used with tolerable frequency on grand occasions by George IV., who dearly loved a pageant, but since the Queen's accession it has seen the light very seldom, and never since the death of the Prince Consort.

The State coach is as beautiful as it is interesting. The body is made of oak very heavily gilded and slung by straps and springs to four magnificently carved tritons of gigantic size. The box-seat, which is of extraordinary dimensions, is supported by the two foremost figures. The celebrated artist, Cipriana, was responsible for the eight delightful panels which decorate the body of the coach. The subjects are mythological and allegorical, and are most delicate in treatment and colouring. A high varnish has kept them in splendid preservation.

The upper part of the coach is of glass, bevelled at the edges. A finely wrought crown makes a fitting ornament to the roof, which is otherwise handsomely decorated with much chased gilt metal work. The body of the coach weighs four tons, and, when in addition to this, the weight of the four huge lamps, the attendants, and the trappings worn by each horse is taken into consideration, it may be imagined that the eight cream-coloured ponies which always drew this wonderful vehicle had enough to do to proceed at a walking pace.

The Queen never liked the State coach, principally on account of the perpetually swinging movement, which made a progress in it most trying. Now, when necessary, she uses the semi-State coach, an exceedingly pretty carriage with a claret-coloured body and a little gilding. This carriage was used by the Queen at the Duke of York's wedding.

Most interesting, perhaps, is the Jubilee landau, a strongly-built, boat-shaped carriage in which the Queen has driven continuously for more than twenty years past. It is a favourite equipage with the Queen, and has been used by her at all kinds of ceremonies in all parts of England. It has no box-seat, and is, in spite of its size, a graceful carriage. It was used by the Queen and the Prince of Wales on Thanksgiving Day in 1872 and on many subsequent occasions. It was completely done up for the great Jubilee procession. The public also saw it on the occasion of the opening of the Imperial Institute.

All the semi-State coaches are painted claret-colour, and are hung on C springs. The other royal carriages are of the same tint, picked out with scarlet, and of an obsolete design. Until a very few years ago the Queen always used to drive in a posting carriage, with a dickey behind, and, indeed, still does so when in Scotland. But in London or at Windsor she now has a coachman on the box, and but for the attendant equerry riding at her wheel, her equipage boasts nothing unusual about it.

The Queen's drives have been many and various, and her conservative instincts still urge her to make every year the same expeditions as she has been accustomed to all

her life.   Many of her drives at Balmoral are arranged on
the posting principle.   Shorter drives to the Danzig Shiel,
along the glens of the Dee and Muick, and into Ballater,
are taken with the Queen's own horses.   When Her
Majesty, either at Balmoral or Windsor, wishes to honour
any one with a call in the course of the afternoon, a groom
is sent over in the morning to apprise the hostess of the
Queen's proposal.   Favourite drives with the Queen when
at Windsor used to be to Ditton to visit the Dowager
Duchess of Buccleuch, and to Mrs. Overstone in Windsor
Forest.

At Osborne the Queen drives chiefly among her own
grounds, where she has eight miles of private roads, only
going sometimes into Cowes.

Our sovereign has had one very serious carriage accident.
It occurred in October, 1863, when, in the first years of her
heavy mourning, she was persuaded by the Princesses Alice
and Helena to drive out from Balmoral to Clova.   It was
past seven and dark when the Royal party, with only John
Brown in attendance, and a little black page boy of
Princess Alice's, started homewards.   The carriage was
completely overturned about two miles from the Alt-na-
guithasach, and though the Princesses were only frightened,
the Queen was much hurt, her face being severely cut and
bruised, and her right hand and thumb injured.   She also
suffered seriously from shock for some days.

The Queen's greatest pleasure now lies in her morning
drives among her gardens in her little basket chair, of which
comfortable conveyances she owns two.   A gillie guides the
pony's head, and one of her grandchildren, either afoot or on
pony back, does escort duty.   Another servant follows behind.
In this quiet way the Queen visits her humbler neighbours
and keeps her memory green about the beautiful spots which
lie on all hands close about her homes.

CHAPTER VIII

THE QUEEN'S FADS AND FANCIES

ALL women are fanciful, and most of them carry their fancies over the border and into the realm of faddism. And so, as it is that our Sovereign is a woman first and a Queen afterwards, she too is beset by little fads and fancies that generally make for old-world simplicity of style, a sweet reverence for past happy times, and a clinging that is touching in its intensity to everything that reflects ever so slightly on the "days that are no more."

One of the Queen's most strongly rooted fancies is a dislike to new faces about her, and that is the reason why so many members of the Royal Household, as well as those servants as she may ever chance to see, grow old and grey in her service. To one in her position the knowledge that she is regarded by new eyes with curiosity is extremely disagreeable.

All domestic servants who have any occasion to enter the Queen's presence have the strictest possible orders on no account to look at Her Majesty. Any servant found infringing this rule is severely reprimanded.

Many of the Queen's fads and fancies are fostered and aided by her marvellous memory, which never allows her to forget the connection between a particular date and a certain thing. Thus, those who have ever been invited to luncheon with the Queen on Sundays will notice that however richly the table may be set forth with massive plate and rare flowers, two small salt-cellars in silver, of a shell design supported by a mermaid, are placed on the table, where Her Majesty can see them. They were given to the Queen many years ago by her faithful attendant, John Brown, and since that day have appeared with unfailing regularity every Sunday morning on the Royal luncheon table.

The Queen also possesses a very elegant small silver soup basin with graceful chased handles and a well modelled setter pointing on the cover. This soup bowl is used only by the Queen when she is unwell, and requires refreshment in her own rooms. But on no account is this bowl ever allowed to go to Balmoral, and equally on no account must it be omitted from the plate-chests that are sent to Osborne. In the same way, out of all the handsome reading lamps and shaded candlesticks that have been made through the years for the Queen, one only is ever used by her—a pretty bedroom candlestick fitted with a clear glass screen. A very elegant silver affair, which holds two candles and is fitted with silver bell shades enamelled green inside, she took a dislike to, and will never have about her, though it was made by her desire after a plan of the Princess Louise. From among the scores of splendid snuffers in the plate rooms, two pairs only are ever used, and these go to Her Majesty's private rooms.

The splendid gold toilette service that decorates the Queen's dressing-room at Windsor never leaves the Castle, neither does the solid gold wash-hand basin which was originally made for Her Majesty's coronation, and which has already, as I have described in a previous chapter, undergone considerable adventures.

It is indeed in many of the more domestic details in life that we discover the Queen to be extremely fanciful and particular. Thus, no gold plate is ever taken to Osborne or Balmoral, and when she takes breakfast in the open air at Frogmore, as she does so often, woe betide the forgetful person who should serve her table with the gold she uses only in her own dining-room at the Castle, or who should omit to place alongside the quaintly-modelled " cock-and-hen " egg-cups the peculiar salt-cellar in blackened silver that Lady Alice Stanley once gave her Royal friend, and which the Queen then said was always to be used under those circumstances.

Her Majesty's conservatism in the arrangement of her own apartments is very touching, particularly when viewed by the light shed by the small cards affixed to the doors of all her rooms in her various residences, which say that everything within was chosen and arranged by her late husband, the Prince Consort, and has to all intents and purposes remained unaltered since his death. To maintain this appearance in the Queen's rooms all the hangings, chintzes, and carpets are accurately copied as it becomes necessary to replace them.

The occasional redecorating of the Queen's private apartments has to be done with the greatest care in order that Her Majesty should not even perceive that they have been more than cleaned. On one occasion while the Queen was away from Windsor an armchair in her private sitting-room was re-stuffed and re-covered. Her Majesty at once ordered it out of her sight on her return, saying it was "too smart."

Most visitors at Windsor will recall the dark iron gates and railings at the top of Castle Hill, inclosing the South Terrace, through which the Queen drives to gain the Upper Ward of the Castle and her private entrance. With a view to pleasing her, these gates and railings were, during an absence of the Court, elaborately gilded at the top. On Her Majesty's return she caught sight of them and at once remarking on the showy effect, ordered that the gilding should be immediately obliterated. An army of painters was summoned, and by the time the Queen left the Castle for her afternoon drive all traces of the garish display had been removed.

A very pretty fancy of the Queen was the sending for the favourite charger of her beloved son-in-law, the Emperor Frederick of Germany, after his death, and stabling it at Windsor, with orders that no one was ever to cross its back again. The horse, which is eighteen hands high, was ridden by the Emperor, when Crown Prince of Germany, in Her Majesty's Jubilee Procession in 1887.

The Queen's love and remembrance of anniversaries is almost proverbial, and those which mark the more sorrowful events of her life are kept as days apart. The 14th December, which date marks the death of the Prince Consort, and ten years later of Princess Alice of Hesse, is observed by the Queen as a day of great mourning. Save at the Memorial Service held at the Albert Mausoleum at Frogmore, not even those members of the Royal family who travel to Windsor for that function see the Queen. No business of any kind is transacted by Her Majesty on that day, she sits almost alone in her own apartments, and it is the one day in the year when, save for the short drive to Frogmore and back, the Queen takes no air. The Court is expected to wear black on this occasion.

Concerning the dress of those about her the Queen is particularly faddy. Etiquette of course governs the form of official or ceremonious garb, but the Ladies-in-Waiting and Maids of Honour have to avoid every kind of snare in the way of extravagant cut, loud colours, or remarkable

style.   For many years even the slightest fringe was
" taboo " at Court, and even now any such adornment has
to be treated with great discretion or earn reprobation from
the Sovereign.   Still it must not be considered that the
Queen is averse to all personal adornment, for she is not.
Her presents to those about her invariably consist of pretty
articles of jewellery or pieces of silk or lace, while at one
time Her Majesty was very fond of going round her gardens
and conservatories and herself selecting the flowers she
wished her ladies to wear in the evening.

About her own clothes the Queen never showed any
particular taste, and nowadays she only fancies the plainest
of gowns and mantles.   Nevertheless, homely in cut as are
Her Majesty's gowns, they are always made of the best
material.   It is an odd fad that induces the Queen to order
every item of her toilette in duplicate.   Most of her clothes
now are made for her by the leading draper at Windsor, and
the order for a cloak, hat or dress, always enumerates two
as the number required.   Her sons and daughters frequently
try to combat Her Majesty's simple tastes, and when the
dress to be worn on the Jubilee day, in 1887, was under
family discussion, the Duke of Connaught cried :

" Now, Mother, you must have something really
smart."

A fancy of the Queen, that no woman will combat, is to
permanently wear on her wrist a bracelet containing the
portrait and hair of the Prince Consort.   A few years ago
the bracelet, from long wear, broke, and had to be sent at
once to Mr. Wagland, the Queen's working jeweller in
Windsor, to be mended.   The Queen's unhappiness and
anxiety during the few hours she was perforce without
the bracelet were quite painful to witness.   Her Majesty's
touching fancy to have a portrait of the Prince Consort
taken after death, and a wreath of immortelles always

fastened at the right-hand side of the head of her bed, is too sacred to be commented on.

One of the Queen's most strongly marked fads is her mania for never destroying anything. This extends not only to her private papers and letters, but even to such ephemeral articles as wearing apparel of the most ordinary kind. Every woman cares for hoarding lace, fur, and feathers, but Her Majesty goes farther than this, and almost without exception, her wardrobe woman can produce the gown, bonnet, or mantle she wore on any particular occasion. The Queen's collection of clothes would form the most accurate and interesting commentary on the modes of the past sixty years. Her Majesty also keeps with great care and pride a large number of articles worn by the late Prince Consort and by her mother the Duchess of Kent.

No one has ever been more portrayed than the Queen ; her features have been reproduced in every known medium. Unlike the majority of her subjects, Her Majesty is very fond of being painted, and makes a perfect sitter, always being composed and patient and yet wearing a pleasing expression. The pictures of the Queen, with statues and busts included, may be numbered by many hundreds, and yet so fond is she of being " taken " that the last new oil painting or the latest photograph is as eagerly anticipated and carefully criticised as though to see the reproduction of her face was quite a novel experience.

Of recent years the Queen's fancy has greatly favoured the photographic art, and it is quite a weakness of hers to be photographed in every possible condition of her daily life. Sitting in her donkey chair, dandling the last new baby, chatting in her private sitting-room among her daughters, working at her writing-table, or breakfasting in the open air, with the Battenberg family and her immediate attendants around her, the Queen's photographer is always to be sent for and ordered to " fix the picture."

This idea of the Queen is not limited by her own personality, but extends to every article in her possession, which in the mass—that is to say, in the various apartments where the things may be kept—as well as singly, are all photographed. Every piece of plate and china, every picture, chair, table, ornament, and articles of even the most trivial description, all pass through the photographer's hands, and are " taken" from every point of view. At Windsor the photographic studio and developing rooms are at the extreme end of the Orangery, which lies beneath the junction of the East and North Terraces, and which opens out on to the sunk East Gardens. Here, under proper escort, have been brought in the course of years every article of Windsor Castle, while as often as not Mr. Cleave, the Queen's private photographer, is sent to Buckingham Palace, Osborne, and Balmoral, to perpetuate the contents of these residences in the same way.

All such photographs are submitted to the Queen, and when she has duly approved of them (and she is most particular about the way in which this branch of photography is executed) they are sent to the department of the Inspector of the Palace, to be arranged in the wonderful bound catalogues, which are another great fad of Her Majesty.

These catalogues are extraordinary affairs, and form in themselves a most remarkable library. Every photo, when affixed to the page, is surrounded by various *data*, which include the number and name of the room in which the article is kept, the number of the article itself, its size, any marks or signs that may be on it, and a full description of it from every point of view. If it is a picture, the artist's name and a description of the frame are added. The number of the negative is kept, and if the article is the Queen's private property, a round stamp to that effect is added to the general description. When the vast quantity of the contents of the Royal Palaces is taken into consideration, it may readily be understood that these catalogues, which have been in course of compilation for several years, and yet which are never really finished, are many in number, large in bulk, and quite one of the most expensive of the Queen's fads. Her Majesty is very fond of her catalogues, and few days pass without her sending for one volume or another.

A well-known prejudice of the Queen is the one she entertains against the re-marriage of widows. On this point Her Majesty is quite immovable, and no arguments have ever been known to even momentarily shake her opinions about this subject.

A strange fact that but few people have ever remarked is that although the walls of the Queen's private apartments are lined with pictures from floor to ceiling, and that portraits of her own children figure largely in the collection, no likenesses of her sons-in-law and daughters-in-law are to be found on the crowded walls. Photographs of her relations by marriage stand about the tables, but the Queen has never placed their portraits on the walls among the pictures which were selected and arranged for her by the late Prince Consort.

All her life the Queen has had a mania for fresh air, and even in the keenest weather the fires are all closely screened, and the temperature of the rooms taken periodically from the small ivory thermometers that, as I have already explained, stand on all the mantelpieces everywhere. Her love for eating in the open air and driving in open carriages is well known.

The Queen's fancy for wax candles as the only medium

for artificial light has of late years been slightly overcome in favour of electric light, but in her own rooms nothing but the finest old-fashioned wax candles is ever used.

Her Majesty's likes and dislikes with regard to persons have always been kept in check by her innate sense of justice and her carefully balanced mind.

The one lamentable exception was her aversion for Lady Flora Hastings, a lady-in-waiting of the Duchess of Kent in 1839. The Queen, who was very young at the time, allowed her prejudices to overcome her judgment, and after various painful scenes, Lady Flora left the Court and soon afterwards died, under circumstances which placed the Queen and her particular friends in the wrong.

Against two of her ablest Ministers, Sir Robert Peel and Benjamin Disraeli, the Queen had the strongest dislikes, but she had occasion in both cases to alter her mind and her fancy, and, indeed, for many years before his death admitted Disraeli (Lord Beaconsfield) to the greatest friendship.

When in Scotland the Queen's kindly fancies turn towards her humbler neighbours, and at christenings and funerals, or where sickness and sorrow are, she may be looked for and found in the tender capacities of consoler and friend.

CHAPTER IX

THE QUEEN'S FORTUNE AND EXPENDITURE, HER CHARITIES AND GIFTS

IN a letter written by Sir Henry Ponsonby, the Queen's Private Secretary, from Aix-les-Bains, on September 18, 1885, addressed to the late Major Ross, then M.P. for Maidstone, he said : " The Queen has bought nothing and possesses nothing in the City of London.   She has invested no money in ground rents, nor does she possess a million to invest.   I refer, of course, solely to the Queen as an individual . . . none of the Queen's own money is, or ever has been, so invested."

With Sir Henry Ponsonby's disclaimer that Her Majesty has never bought land within the confines of the City of London, I have nothing to do.   It is rather his statement that in 1885 (twelve years ago) the Queen did not own a million of private money, that is interesting.   If Sir Henry Ponsonby were alive now he would scarcely stand by such an assertion, for almost every year that has passed since 1885 has witnessed a curtailage of Her Majesty's expenditure and a vast increment to her savings.   The one exceptional period was in 1887, the Jubilee Year, when the most lavish entertaining was indulged in, and immense sums were spent in all directions.

Before entering into the more private sources of Her

Majesty's yearly income—from which it should be remembered that she is at liberty to save what she can—it may be as well to consider the allowance granted her by the country, and to roughly jot down the manner in which this £385,000 a year is spent. The sums will serve as standards of comparison, if they answer no other purpose. From the country, then, the Queen is allowed for her Privy Purse, £60,000 ; for expenses of the household, £172,500 ; for salaries and retiring allowances, £131,260 ; and for Royal Bounty, Alms, and Special Service, £13,200. These sums leave unappropriated £8,040. It is worthy of note that with this identical allowance, George IV. and William IV. had no unappropriated money at the end of the year.

In addition to this sum, the Queen, when she came to the throne, secured a grant of £8,000 a year for her mother, the Duchess of Kent, while after her marriage the Prince Consort had a separate allowance of £30,000. The Queen wished the Prince to have £100,000, but Lord Melbourne persuaded her to only ask the country for £50,000. Her Majesty was much annoyed at the further reduction of the allowance. So soon as the Princes came of age, suitable grants were made to them, while on their marriages the Princesses were voted incomes of £4,000 a year. These figures are merely given to show that so far as the Civil List is concerned, the Sovereign has the individual disposal of almost every shilling of it. In detail the Civil List is a wonderful document. Every item of expense is mentioned and provided for. Tradesmen's bills, the department of the Master of the Horse, the Royal Wardrobe, pensions, salaries, and gratuities are all duly mentioned. Every imaginable want, whether to eat, drink, wear, or give away, has certain sums set down for it. Hence it is that the splendid income from the Duchy of Lancaster, which property and title belong to the reigning Sovereign of Great

Britain by private right, and as an appurtenance from the Crown, is paid directly into the Privy Purse, and Her Majesty can save or spend it as she pleases.

The Duchy of Lancaster, which has meads, forests, chases, and woods in thirteen counties, belonged originally to Saxon nobles who rose against the Norman Conqueror. Their estates were confiscated, and in 1265 were in the possession of Robert Ferrers, Earl of Derby. This nobleman took part with Simon de Montfort in his rebellion, and was deprived of all his estates in 1265 by Henry III., who bestowed them on his youngest son, Edmund, Earl of Lancaster. From him dates the connection between royalty and the duchy. In 1310, Thomas, second son of Lancaster, son of Edmund, married a great heiress, the only child of De Lacy, Earl of Lincoln. By this alliance he became the wealthiest and the most powerful subject of the Crown, possessing in right of himself and his wife six earldoms. In 1311 he became involved in the combination formed by several nobles to induce the King to part with Piers Gaveston. Edward II. was at first highly incensed, but ultimately pardoned the conspirators, including the Earl of Lancaster. That very imprudent personage subsequently took up arms against his Sovereign and was beheaded.

In 1326 an act was passed for reversing the attainder of Earl Thomas in favour of his brother Henry, Earl of Lancaster. Earl Henry left a son. The son was surnamed "Grismond," from the place of his birth. He greatly distinguished himself in the French war under Edward III., and was the second knight companion of the Order of the Garter, Edward the "Black Prince" being the first. Edward III. created him, about 1348, Duke of Lancaster, and the county of Lancaster was formed into a palatinate. This great nobleman died in 1361, leaving two daughters to

inherit his vast possessions ; but on the death of the elder
without issue, the whole devolved on the second, Blanche,
who married John of Gaunt, son of Edward III.   He was
created Duke of Lancaster, played a prominent part in
history, and died in 1399, leaving a son by Blanche—Henry
Plantagenet, surnamed Boling-Broke, from Bullingbrook
Castle, in Lincolnshire, the scene of his birth.   He became
King Henry IV., and thus the duchy merged in the Crown.

The Queen's revenue from this source has been steadily
increasing.   Thus in 1865 it was £26,000 ; in 1867,
£29,000 ; in 1869, £31,000 ; in 1872, £40,000.

A second source of income which the Queen held until
the Prince of Wales came of age—when it was, according
to precedence, made over to his Royal Highness—is the
Duchy of Cornwall, the estates of which lie in Devon,
Somerset, Wilts, Surrey, and London.   The Duchy had
been at the time of the Queen's accession hopelessly mis-
managed, and it was owing to the Prince Consort's untiring
energy that his eldest son's heritage was at all worth having.
In 1824 the gross revenue had fallen to £22,000 ; in 1872
it was nearly £70,000.   When the Prince of Wales came
of age, instead of having from £13,000 to £14,000 a
year from his Duchy, as the last Prince of Wales had,
there was a revenue of £50,000 a year clear, and cash
enough to buy Sandringham.   The income is now increasing
at the rate of about £3,000 a year, on the average.

Far more romantic, however, than the incomes from long-
settled heritages can ever be, is the origin of the greater
portion of Her Majesty's great wealth.   On the 30th of
August, 1852, there died a penurious old gentleman of
seventy-two.   John Camden Nield was the son of a goldsmith who had executed work for George III., and kept a
shop in St. James's Street.   The old jeweller was in his way
a great philanthropist, and emulated Howard in his attempt

to ameliorate the condition of those poor wretches who languished in His Majesty's prisons. He sent his son to Trinity College, Cambridge, and the bar, and at his death left him £250,000. This great sum John Camden Nield saved and invested, living himself in a most miserly fashion. When his will was opened it was found that with the exception of a few legacies he had left his fortune of £500,000, to "Her Most Gracious Majesty, Queen Victoria, begging Her Majesty's most gracious acceptance of the same, for her sole use and benefit, and that of her heirs." The Queen sought out Nield's relations and gave them £1,000 each, and raised a monument to his memory.

This splendid sum Her Majesty has left practically untouched, and it must now have accumulated to a £1,000,000. The Queen also inherited from her husband, who was of a most careful and businesslike disposition, a large part of the £600,000 he left behind him.

It was in her comparatively poor days that Her Majesty purchased the greater portion of the Osborne Estate. She had originally hoped to buy Norris Castle, where she had stayed in her childhood, but was obliged to give it up as she said she "could not afford it." A little later Balmoral was bought and the Castle built. Both these private properties of the Queen have been added to very largely from time to time, and their value is yearly increasing. Osborne is now reckoned as being five times as valuable as when it was purchased in 1844.

The Queen had another stroke of luck in 1881, when, by the advice of Lord Cross, Lord Sidney, and the late Sir Arnold White, her solicitor, she bought outright some property for £78,000. The market value of that purchase is now reckoned at about £170,000.

According to the new Doomsday Book, Her Majesty owns, privately, some 37,372 acres of land which yields a yearly income of between £20,000 and £25,000. The return would be higher, but that much of the acreage is Scottish moor and forest lands. The Queen owns three very fine forests. They are those of Balmoral, part of the original estate bought from the Fife trustees in 1851, Ballochbine, acquired by Her Majesty from the late Colonel Farquharson, of Invercauld, in 1878, and Abergeldie. The deer in these forests are most valuable animals.

Claremont was granted to the Queen for her life in 1866, with a reversion to the country at what all her subjects pray may be the distant day of her death, but in 1882 Her Majesty bought it from the Crown. Of property abroad the Queen possesses land and houses at Coburg, and one of the most magnificent villas at Baden, which was left to the Queen by a Princess of the house of Hohenlohe.

It must not be concluded, however, that the vast fortune of Queen Victoria has merely dropped into her hands, or rolled itself up. Economy with sufficiency has been the watchword of Her Majesty's career, and during the " 40's," when every year the most gorgeous entertainments were perpetually being given to crowned heads, and for the good of trade and the circulation of money at the Royal palaces, the ministers of state used frequently to boast of the wonderful management which could do things so royally and yet never ask the country for a penny-piece.

Invested money and land do not form the limits to the Queen's possessions ; far from it.

No monarch can point to such a mass of valuables as were presented to Her Majesty's private person at the time of her first Jubilee, and though much of the gold and silver plate at Windsor is, like the Crown jewels, Crown property, the Queen can claim nearly half a million pounds'-worth as her own. Her private collection of jewels is also very valuable, while her laces, of which she is extremely proud, are worth very many thousands of pounds.

Her own pictures and statuary hold perhaps a value that is more sentimental than monetary, though many of her Landseers would fetch heavy prices; but much of the china she has purchased, *bibelots*, carvings, bronzes, and knick-knacks, are intrinsically worth a very great deal.

The Queen's perquisites are, with few exceptions, now-adays more interesting than valuable, and comprise some strange articles. The upper half of every whale captured on the coast of Great Britain and Ireland belongs to the Queen, as also does every sturgeon caught. Tailors holding an appointment to the Queen should present her with a silver needle every year. The yearly perquisites of a table-cloth, a white dove, a curry-comb, a white hare, a knife, a nightcap, scarlet stockings, and crossbows, are not now exacted. The Dukes of Marlborough and Wellington present the Queen on each anniversary of the battles of Blenheim and Waterloo with small replicas of the French flag and Royal English Standard. At the end of each year the flags are given to the officer of the Guard who is on duty on those two days. The most valuable perquisites received by the Queen are six magnificent Cashmere shawls, from Cashmere, which range in value from £100 to £250 each.

With the charities which emanate from the Civil List we have little to do. They are much regulated by precedent, and are mostly set forth and arranged by the Queen's Private Secretary. But of that truer charity that is known only by the recipient, that is not blazoned in newspapers, nor talked of at Court, what is to be said? Nothing, and yet everything. It comes freely and unostentatiously from the Queen's ever-open private purse, often it is bestowed with words of womanly sympathy and humble gladness that she can do good. It commands no gratitude, asks for no thanks. The stream of it is wide and deep, and it is always flowing. It is too much the fashion nowadays to sneer at the Queen's charity. To do so is to betray a gross ignorance of facts, or a wilful blindness to the truth. Her Majesty's charity is simply immense, and comprises every known form of assistance and aid. Yet the public know little or nothing of this, for the Queen's right hand is ignorant of the doings of her left. Just as she bought the poor beaten donkey "Jacko" from his cruel Niçois master, she will give the first encouragement to a struggling artist, put the sick in the way of health, and give back to the down-trodden and wretched their self-respect. The Queen's charity is as beautiful as the rest of her character ; tender and retiring, just and generous.

The Queen's presents take every form. From time to time she has given large sums of money as gifts. Many of her splendidly-married grand-daughters have had to thank Her Majesty for their costly *trousseaux* and wonderful jewels. Her presents to the Duchess of York on her marriage were magnificent, for the Queen is very open-handed in such matters. Of gifts to her household and dependents at Christmas time she is very lavish, and she never forgets a birthday or the style of present that would be most acceptable. Her ladies often receive handsome jewels from her, while her wedding presents to brides in whom she takes interest seldom, if ever, stop at the cus-tomary Cashmere shawl. Where children are concerned her generosity is boundless, and every child on her great estates spends a happier Christmas for the toys from the Castle.

Yet in the giving of presents, as in all, the Queen is ruled by a wise discretion. She knows that when the day comes on which she must doff her crown and lay down her sceptre, however large a fortune she may leave behind, there will be many who will have a just claim to a share of it.

The Duke of Connaught is not rich, neither is Princess Christian, and both have families. The young Duke of Albany's future depends greatly on the Queen's beneficence, and though Princess Henry of Battenberg will be a woman of property, she has four little ones to settle in a becoming station. Whatever the Queen elects to do with her property and money it will be right. But no one beyond the circle of her family and legal advisers will ever know the real contents of her will, for the wills of those who are royal are never proved.

CHAPTER X

THE QUEEN'S PASTIMES

THE Queen is a great believer in the homely proverb that "all work and no play make Jack a dull boy," and all through her hardworking life she has always made time for a little relaxation—or at any rate a change of occupation, for Her Majesty is too essentially an active-minded woman to ever take more rest than comes to her in the course of her afternoon drive.

First claim on the Queen's few moments of leisure is won by games of cards of the commonplace and sociable order that are in vogue in every happy English family. In days when the Court was livelier than it is now, the Queen always started a round game of cards after dinner, when there were no State visitors present, and frequently those members of the Household who were not on duty would be sent for to make up a tableful, for the young Queen was childishly fond of a merry party.

On these occasions "Vingt-et-un," "Pope Joan," and "Nainjaune," were generally played, and always for small sums of money. Court etiquette demands that all coin of the realm passed to the Sovereign shall be new and unused, and the Ladies-in-Waiting and Maids of Honour who joined in these games were always obliged to keep new money about them.

That the stakes were not high is evidenced by a favourite Maid of Honour, who boasts that on one evening she made the great haul of *eightpence !*

Whist (with or without a dummy) was a very favourite game with Prince Albert, and whenever the Queen and he went on their quiet little excursions among the Highlands, or retired for a few days' absolute repose to their dear little " bothie " at Alt-na-Guithasach with only a Maid of Honour and some servants for retinue, a pack of cards was always put in the baggage, and two or three rubbers of whist would be the order of the evening. Of chess, too, Her Majesty was very fond, and she played it, for one of her sex—who are not as a rule good at mastering the game—exceedingly well. In the Green Drawing-room at Windsor there is an exquisite chess-table, inlaid most richly with coloured marbles, while among the Queen's possessions there must also be reckoned a wonderful set of chessmen of lavish Eastern design, worked out in solid gold and silver. Besides these charming incentives to the game, there are in all the Royal palaces several very beautiful inlaid chess boards as well as most valuable tables in carving and inlay for cards.

A constant companion of the Queen in all her travels, even to being granted a place in her yacht cabin and railway saloon, is a specially made specimen of the very clever " Patience Table " invented some years ago by Lady Adelaide Cadogan. Games of " Patience " nowadays form the Queen's principal and dearest recreation. Prince Albert was an adept at any intricate games, and it was he who taught them to the Queen. All through her life she has played " Patience " under various conditions, and on the occasion when Her Majesty visited Sir Robert Peel at Drayton Manor, we are told that the Queen, looking very pretty in a pink silk dress with three flounces, played "Patience" the whole evening with the ladies of the assembled party.

The Queen plays "Patience" a great deal during her railway journeys, among her favourite games being "The Harp" and "The Fan." Her cards are specially made for her, and are rather smaller than the usual size. Each packet is inclosed in a case of scarlet morocco stamped with the Queen's cipher. But if the Queen is happy amusing herself, she is equally pleased to applaud the efforts of others who try to amuse her. She will find as much delight in dressing a Christmas tree (a task she always performed with her own hands) as in attending a Hallowe'en gathering, a Highland function of which she was very fond. The first time Her Majesty ever witnessed the picturesque spectacle she was so delighted with it that the following year—1867—she took an active part in the celebration herself. The Queen, with Princess Louise, Prince Leopold, and Lady Ely, returned earlier than usual from their drive to take part in the procession, which on this occasion consisted of the Queen, her children, the household, and all the gillies on the Balmoral estate. The whole party walked round the house and grounds, every one carrying a torch, which was afterwards flung on a bonfire to blaze while the gillies danced reels to Ross the piper's playing. The quaintness and weirdness of the sight may be easily imagined, and the pleasure it gave to those taking part in it.

The Queen also derived great amusement from the Highland gatherings, and used to grow most excited over the various games of "Throwing the Hammer," "Putting the Stone," and the racing. Once at a gathering at Braemar to which the Queen took the Duchess of Kent, she was vastly delighted that her gillie Duncan won a most difficult race from among a great number of other clansmen. It was to commemorate the pleasure the Queen has derived from these simple country pastimes, that the exquisite figures in solid gold, which so often adorn the Royal dinner-table, of Highlanders engaged in their national games, were made.

In the Queen's youth *La Grace* was a fashionable game, but Her Majesty openly admires the more active game of tennis, at which the Duke of Connaught, Princess Henry of Battenberg, and several of the Household are adepts. The tennis courts, both of grass and asphalte, are excellent at Windsor—where they are just below the East Terrace— and at Osborne, where they lie to the left of the Avenue, and behind the reservoir. Her Majesty is very fond of watching a game of tennis, and is a keen critic of style and play.

It is on the pleasance below the East Terrace at Windsor that Buffalo Bill and his troupe once presented their show to the equal delight and wonderment of the Royal grand-children and their august grandmother, who made the most sympathetic audience in the world.

Here, also, one of the Queen's Indian attendants is accustomed to give exhibitions of "tent pegging," picking up the handkerchief, and other feats of daring and fine riding, all of which Her Majesty views with great pleasure. Sometimes very promiscuous entertainers are bidden to the Castle, generally, it must be understood, at the request of the young Princes of Battenberg. On one occasion a pair of dancing bears was enthusiastically applauded, while at another time a "Punch and Judy" gave intense pleasure to the Queen. Once the little Princess Ena caught sight of a monkey in Windsor Town, and the owner thereof was, with his barrel organ and animal, immediately commanded to play in the Quadrangle beneath the windows of the Oak Dining-room. The Queen was much amused when the monkey climbed the portico and tried to find a way into the Castle through the dining-room windows.

It is with such simple pastimes as these, homely amusements about which the great public never hear, that our beloved Sovereign has preserved her young heart and cheerful disposition, and she derived as much joy from Henglers' circus when it gave a performance a few years ago in the Great Riding School as she ever has from the lavish entertainments that great London managers have placed before her. It was after witnessing this circus show that Her Majesty, who had been greatly entertained with the quaint antics of Whimsical Walker's extraordinary donkey, expressed a strong desire to make that learned animal's acquaintance. The donkey was duly brought forward, and the Queen proceeded to touch him with her ebony stick, whereupon the creature turned round and began to lash out most savagely at Her Majesty, who, when she had recovered from her natural alarm, remarked to those about her: "I fear he is not a very loyal subject."

The Queen was always fond of playing with her children and learning games which she afterwards taught them. The Hon. Georgiana Liddell—one of her Maids of Honour in her early married life—first won Court favour by teaching her Royal Mistress to make a mouse out of a pocket-handkerchief, and to cause it to run about her arm and hand.

Her Majesty takes delight in a clever riddle or rebus, but on one occasion she was very angry at having been hoaxed over a riddle which was sent to her with a letter to the effect that it had been made by the Bishop of Salisbury. For four days the Queen and Prince Albert sought for the reply, when Charles Murray (Controller of the Household) was directed to write to the bishop and ask for the solution. The answer received was that the bishop had not made the riddle nor could he solve it.

Until the Prince Consort's death, the Queen when in town went to the theatre and opera about three times a week; both being pastimes of which she was very fond. Also she very frequently commanded theatrical companies to Windsor.

Performances at that time were nearly always given in the Rubens Room, where hang the famous portraits of Rubens and Helena Forman, his second wife, and the great picture of " St. Martin and the Beggar." Owing to lack of space, few beyond Royalties and their households were ever invited. Christmas time was the great period for these entertainments, and the sequence of these delightful evenings was only broken in 1850 by the death of Queen Adelaide, in 1855 by the universal anxiety about the English troops in the Crimea, and in 1858 by the marriage of the Princess Royal, but in this last case other entertainments were arranged.

In all, some thirty-two plays were performed during those years, and among those who acted before the Queen privately were Charles Kean, who played eleven times; Mrs. Kean, eight times; Webster, seven times; Charles Matthews, five times; the popular Keeleys, ten times; and Buckstone, on three occasions. Phelps also played Henry V. at Windsor on Thursday, November 10th, 1853.

It was to please the Queen that Charles Kemble returned to the stage on March 24th, 1840, and four following nights.

After December 14th, 1861, however, all was changed, and until the Prince of Wales persuaded Her Majesty to witness a performance of *The Colonel* by a company travelling through Scotland, the Queen had seen no theatrical representation since her bereavement. Even then it was some years again before the Princes and Princesses were permitted to amuse themselves with the getting up of plays and *tableaux vivants*, but recently these have been most frequent at Balmoral in the autumn, and Osborne at Christmas time. The Queen takes immense interest in these quite "private theatricals," and the dresses, casting of parts, and make-up are all deferred to her kindly experience, while she makes a point of being at every rehearsal. Both in the Ball-room at Balmoral and in the splendid Indian-room at Osborne, stage and proper lighting apparatus are easily fixed. It is noteworthy that at these little entertainments, ordinary dinner dress only is worn, jewels are considered bad style, and the list of guests comprise few beyond the members of the Court and Household and the upper servants.

At Windsor, things are on a larger scale. The curious cabin-shaped Waterloo Gallery, which was built for William IV. (over an old courtyard once called the Horn Court) in 1830 by Sir Jeffrey Wyatville, makes an excellent theatre—in fact, so good, that the temporary stage which was put up under the auspices of the late Sir Augustus Harris for the production of *Carmen* has been allowed to remain.

The Waterloo Chamber, which is over ninety feet long, contains thirty-eight pictures, principally portraits of kings, admirals, statesmen, generals, mostly from the brush of Sir Thomas Lawrence, who surpassed himself in his work for George IV., though there are also specimens of the work of Beechey, Wilkie, Pickersgill, and Shee. The cornice is oddly decorated with gilt gargoyles and brown monkeys' heads. Six splendid oil lamps on handsome supports and five magnificent crystal chandeliers light the apartment.

The stage, which is raised five feet from the floor level, and the proscenium are draped in crimson and gold. They face the gallery. At a performance, the orchestra is literally embowered in palms and flowers from the Frogmore gardens, which also are used to fringe the edge of the crimson-covered platform, four feet high, on which the Queen and other Royalties and the Household sit in chairs of crimson and gold. It is noteworthy that the well-raised seats behind the Royal platform are carpeted in dove-coloured cloth, as being distinct from the Royal red square reserved to Royalty, and that the chairs are smaller and of white and red. The Gallery at the end of the apartment and opposite the stage, is filled by the head servants.

The Queen always enters after all the company—even her own family—is seated. A gently raised slope obviates the necessity of her mounting any steps. The Indian attendants and those who are in waiting accompany Her Majesty, who sits a little forward from the rest of her guests in a low armchair. A footstool is before her, and a small table holds her fan, opera-glasses, programme, and book of the words. The applause is always led by the Queen, who taps either her hand or table with her fan. The *coup d'œil* from this little stage is very magnificent, for not only is the apartment brilliantly lit, but full dress is worn. The Household is in uniform, and decorated with orders, while the scarlet liveries of the Royal servants make a fine show as they hand refreshments from time to time, the gala dresses of the Indians are picturesque among the palms, and the burnished helmets and shoulder-plates of the firemen, who are always present at such functions, go to make up a splendid sight.

The Queen retires first of all the company, and after graciously thanking the performers goes straight to her own rooms.

On these occasions the Guard Chamber and St. George's Hall are transformed by means of curtains and screens into dressing-rooms for the actors, while the ladies use the Throne Room and the Queen's Closet. Supper is laid in the Presence Chamber for the chief performers and the Gentlemen of the Household, while the supers, carpenters, and stage hands sit in the Vandyke Room, and the orchestra in the Audience Chamber.

The money paid by the Queen for large theatrical entertainments does not pretend to compensate a manager for his outlay, but, on the other hand, it should not be forgotten that the Royal purse is heavily taxed on these occasions. An army of skilled workpeople are fed and paid at the Castle for days before and after the performance. The theatrical troupe are treated *en prince* when they arrive, and the hospitality shown them is boundless.

At the same time, public speculation has always been rife as to what sums are really paid to managers for their efforts to entertain Her Majesty. It may at once be said that when, some four years ago, Sir Augustus Harris first received the Queen's command to produce operas at Windsor Castle, the honour done him and the accompanying advertisement were as valuable as the cheque always paid. Within a year or so, however, the performances, at Windsor became so frequent, and so many different managers and companies appeared there, that Sir Augustus represented to the Queen's Private Secretary that, as the advertisement had ceased to be exclusive, the emolument received by him could not be considered sufficient compensation for the painting of special scenes, the rehearsing of artists, orchestra, and supers, their extra payment, and their transport to and from Windsor. The case was laid before the Queen, and the next performance organised for her by Sir Augustus Harris was paid for at an increased and more profitable rate.

These true facts of the Queen's most reasonable wish to

make adequate compensation for her pastimes go far to disprove the credibility—if indeed any contradiction were now needed—of the scandalous statements once made by Douglas Jerrold in *Lloyd's* newspaper with regard to the payment of actors who appeared before the Queen.

The affair, which happened at the time that Charles Kean was " Master of the Revels " at Court (a part for which he was chosen by the Queen in 1848), first got wind through a subordinate actor, who had lately appeared in a small part at Windsor, one day appearing in a police court and offering the presiding magistrate, as a contribution to the poor box, the paltry sum of a few shillings and some odd pence, saying that it was his fee for acting before the Queen. Much comment was made, and Jerrold worked himself into a white heat over the matter, which gave the Queen the deepest annoyance and pain. It was subsequently proved that the payment of the actors, as well as the engaging of them, was intrusted to Charles Kean, who cut down prices and filled his pockets at Her Majesty's expense.

CHAPTER XI

THE QUEEN'S SERVANTS

NEARLY the most charming and womanly phase of the Queen's character is displayed in her relationship to her servants. Of course, all her subjects are her obedient servants, and the greatest grandee of all her large household is bound to render her loyal and faithful service, and indeed does so cheerfully. But I would now speak of those humbler beings whom the average man and woman treat as mere menials, but who are, in the eyes of Her Majesty, fellow creatures and friends. There are few people in the world who have received such kindnesses from the Queen as her servants, and few who regard her with more sincere devotion and admiration.

And, indeed, the Queen's servants should be faithful to her, for she stands by and protects them to the last. The small lodges at Windsor, Osborne, and Claremont, and the many cosy cottages at Balmoral are filled by men and women who have grown grey in the service of the Royal family. It is the same at Hampton Court, her palaces in London, and houses at Richmond and Kew. Wherever the Queen has any personal jurisdiction and a post or home to give, there may be found old retainers who have served not only her own gracious self, but any member of her family. The Royal gardens and kitchens, laundries, farms, and stables are full of such ancient folk, many of whom remember the Queen as an infant, and whose only talk is of the beneficence of their beloved Royal mistress.

One of the quaintest of these old servitors was Jonathan Mace, who was two years old at the time of George III.'s jubilee. He had been a day labourer at Frogmore in the Duchess of Kent's employ. At the Duchess' death the Queen took upon herself the pensioning of all those of her mother's servants as she did not draft directly into her own service. Mace was retained as a help in the Frogmore gardens, and could tell some comic stories of the young Princes and Princesses and the pranks they used to play. Without in the least meaning any intentional disrespect he always spoke of the Queen's spirited sons as "rare young toads," and of his first mistress, the Duchess of Kent, as "the old gal." In his later years he kept the tiny lodge at the entrance of the Frogmore Gardens, receiving 16s. a week and perquisites for his trouble. He wore the uniform of Her Majesty's lodge-keepers, namely, a green plush coat and waistcoat, the collar bound with gold braid, black trousers, a tall hat, and brass buttons with V.R. upon them.

The Duchess of Kent's lady-in-waiting, Lady Augusta Bruce, of whom the Queen always spoke as "dear Augusta," was also taken into the Royal household as a kind of lady secretary.

It is noticeable that the Queen always brought up her children to treat servants with consideration and fairness. The Princess Royal, who, as a child, was rather overbearing in her manner, was frequently punished by the Queen for rudeness and sharp speaking to the domestics, while on one occasion the Duke of York, when a lad, was severely reprimanded by Her Majesty before a number of people for some inconsiderate remark he made to a servant. The result of her wise training is that the Royal Family make the best masters and get the best servants in the world. Unless a domestic quits any of the Royal households on marriage or by his own wish, he is certain of good wages all his working days and an ample pension afterwards. And of even more than that, for never yet was there a dependent on the Queen or her family who was not certain of cheery words in times of trouble and kindly greetings always. Until the day of her death the Prince of Wales would visit his old nurse, while the young Duchess of York never omits, when she is at White Lodge, to go and see those humble folk who were kind to her in childhood. Many of the most loving and thankful words ever added by Her Majesty's own hand to the *Court Circular* have been tributes of esteem and gratitude to some good servant who has " gone before."

At the same time it must not be thought that the Queen is a weak mistress. Far from it. The service she exacts is always most responsible, and she desires that it should be performed punctually and well. She is, herself, far too thorough and hardworking a servant of her State and her People not to appreciate and expect the firstfruits of every one's powers. Whatever is done in her service for her wages must be done with all the might. The Queen is a strictly just and honourable woman and expects justice and honour from those about her, from the highest even to the lowest.

As a rule, however, such domestic differences and back-stair bickerings as must arise from time to time in all large establishments are laid before a little Court composed of the higher officers of the Household, who go carefully to the root of every quarrel and complaint, and who give judgment upon them—all such cases and judgments being, if serious, laid before the Queen herself. The institution is a strange one, but it works admirably, and the servants, knowing the absolute fairness of the arrangement, are more than content to be governed by it.

That rules for the guidance of the Royal servants were deemed necessary and existed so far back as Charles I.'s time is shown by an old black letter document which hangs in the great Servants' Hall at Windsor Castle. It is headed:—

"Twelve good rules found in the study of Charles I. of blest memory."

> Profane no divine ordinances.
> Touch no State matters.
> Urge no healths.
> Pick no quarrels.
> Maintain no ill opinions.
> Encourage no vice.
> Repeat no grievances.
> Reveal no secrets.
> Make no comparisons.
> Keep no bad company.
> Make no long meals.
> Lay no wagers.
> "These rules observed will maintain
> Thy peace and everlasting gain."

The Servants' Hall at Windsor is a magnificent apartment with a Gothic roof, and is the most imposing of all the Servant's Halls among the Royal residences.

More modern rules for the guidance of the Queen's servants have been drawn up from time to time, but save in detail they differ little from the arrangements made by the Queen, Prince Consort, and the Baroness Lehzen quite early in the reign. The chief of these rules is that no servant is permitted in any part of the Castle to which he or she is not accredited ; thus those who clean the State Rooms may not go to the Private Apartments, while an exclusive and most trustworthy staff are told off for the Queen's Private Suite. In the Queen's own rooms, it is her " dressers," of whom two are always on duty at a time, who are mainly responsible for Her Majesty's personal comfort and for the tidiness of the suite. It is their duty to arrange the flowers, to see each day that every article is in the place the Queen likes best, and to be immediately at hand. They are, in fact, highly trained and efficient maids, and they are always about the person of the Sovereign, one always sleeping within easy call of Her Majesty.

The Queen has always been much attached and extremely kind to her dressers. Of more than one she has painted the likeness, and the portrait of Annie M'Donald, a great favourite, that hangs in the Queen's rooms, is an excellent piece of work. Jane Shackle, a wardrobe maid, and a daughter of one of the Queen's pages, was also a most trusted servant. She travelled with her Royal mistress and party on the famous pseudonymous expedition to Glen Fishie and Granton in September, 1860, when the whole party put up at a little village inn, and had the dinner served by the landlady in ringlets.

Another most excellent servant to the Queen was her coachman, Wagland, whose connection with the Royal Family was quite extraordinary. His grandfather entered George III.'s household in 1788 ; his father was for sixty years in the Royal service, thirty-two years being passed as a porter at the Royal Mews at Windsor. Wagland himself became a Royal servant in 1831, was for seventeen years a postillion, and in 1857 was made Queen's coachman. His daughter was nurserymaid to the Prince of Wales' children. Surely a sufficiently wonderful record in these days of decadent domestic service.

It is this old-world fashion of keeping whole families together that has secured to the Queen and her children such excellent servants. They are, as it were, born into the business, and as they never mix with other classes of domestics, they are uncontaminated by the too frequently muddy stream from which commoner folk are compelled to draw their household helps. Once this fact is grasped it ceases to astonish when one finds Grants, Browns, McDonalds, and Clarks in every branch of the Queen's domestic service.

Of all the Queen's servants, John Brown, who was born at "The Bush," a small farm north of Balmoral Castle, and who began life as a stable lad at Balmoral, was the most remarkable. Of rugged exterior and singularly uncourtly manners, he from the first commended himself to the Prince Consort, who made him a gillie, and in 1849 a personal outdoor attendant on himself and the Queen. In 1851 his services were exclusively demanded by the Queen when on expedition and jaunts in Scotland, and it was John Brown and John Grant, the head keeper, who were always taken on the secret trips of Her Majesty and the Prince. It is recorded of these two brawny Scotchmen that on arrival at some very poor inn they were commanded to wait on their Royal mistress at meals, but being too shy they deputed their duties to a woman of the village.

The sayings and doings of John Brown were many and quaint. He was of the stuff of which the king's jesters were made in the olden times. He was very blunt in speech, and never gave way to the whims or fancies of any one, not even excepting the Queen herself. He was not at all above reproving Her Majesty for any sartorial economy she might exercise, and would often tell her that her cloak was too old or her bonnet too shabby. Once in Scotland, after a picnic luncheon taken at the Glassalt Shiel, the Queen asked for a table to be brought from the cottage at which she could sit and make some sketches. Table after table failed to suit the Queen's taste, and the servants were at their wits' end. Suddenly Brown awoke to the situation, picked up one of the discarded tables, planted it before the Queen, and said:

" It'n na possible to mak' anither table for you up here."

The Queen admitted the common-sense of Brown's remark and used the table.

His bluntness, however, was greatly resented by many of the Queen's relations, and there are many stories told of his curt speeches to the Prince of Wales, and others of the Royal family. Many of the Court officials did not like him and more than once there was some intriguing to displace him. But the Queen appreciated to the full that loyalty and singleness of heart that saved her life from the would-be regicide O'Connor in 1872, and that so frequently stood between her and the impertinence of vulgar sightseers.

Among his fellow servants John Brown was greatly beloved. They found him rough, uneducated, and a stern disciplinarian, but strictly just. He would always take the weaker side in a dispute, and obtained justice for all the servants from the committee that, as I have shown, quietly rules the Queen's household. He was honest and trustworthy, and a good fellow among his peers, and for all his undoubted influence, never became an upstart. A failing, which the kindly Queen refused to recognise, beset him in his later years, but his death caused genuine sorrow in the Servants' Hall, where his portrait now hangs, as in the

Queen's drawing-room. A servant's tribute to his memory was : " I am very sorry he is dead. It would be better for us all if he were still alive."

All Brown's brothers passed into the Queen's service. Donald Brown went to Osborne, Hugh became Keeper of the Kennels at Windsor, James Brown was the shepherd at Balmoral, and Archibald Brown was made a page in the Royal household. The Clarks were cousins of the Browns, and Francie Clark took John Brown's place as personal attendant to the Queen after his death. Francie himself is dead now, and his brother has his post. The Grants have also held positions in the Royal Family as valets, messengers, and keepers. John Grant's daughter is housekeeper at Balmoral.

Promotion is the order of the Queen's household, and the humblest may in time rise to posts of great responsibility and excellent wages. In fact, the possibilities among the Queen's domestics are many and good. The health and happiness of the Queen's servants are amply provided for. Dr. Ellison, at Windsor, can always be seen by any domestic at the Castle, and often the Queen sends her own body physician, Sir James Reid, to those who are very ill. Their amusements are always encouraged by Her Majesty. The upper servants are invariably invited to witness the theatricals and *tableaux*, dances are given at Balmoral under the management of the factor, whilst at Christmas there are presents, Christmas trees, and entertainments for all.

The Queen's Indian servants have every facility granted them for following their own mode of life and ways of eating.

It has been a subject of frequent complaint in certain quarters that most of the Queen's servants are Scotch. Why should they not be ? Her Majesty has found them loyal, honest, silent, and trustworthy. She surely does well to form her domestic household from such excellent material.

Only the Queen's more intimate personal attendants move from place to place with the Court ; the large bulk of the establishment remains always in the different palaces.

CHAPTER XII

THE QUEEN'S WALKS

LOOKING back at the Queen's long life, and considering her arduous duties both of State and Society, her
frequent condition—during many years—of delicate health,
and the little spare time that was ever really at her command,
it is extraordinary to remember that Her Majesty was ever an
enthusiastic and intrepid walker, and that she herself
attributes much of her strength and ability for work to her
equal capacity for taking outdoor and active exercise.

In London, of course, it never has been possible for the
Queen, since her accession, to go a-foot, save in the fine
gardens that lie at the back of Buckingham Palace, for,
fond of walking as Her Majesty is, she could never with
safety have faced the crowds that would have dogged her
footsteps.   It was nothing beyond the scandalous mobbing
to which she was subjected when she went for a few days'
change of air to Brighton, in February, 1842, that caused
the Queen to vow she would never set foot in that town
again.

She also complained much of the gardens of the
Pavilion, where she stayed.   They were small, low, and
very damp, and possessed the insuperable objection of being
overlooked by numbers of houses, so that it was impossible
for any of the Court to take an airing in them.

So annoyed was Her Majesty while there, and so insuperable a dislike did she take to the place, that she at once determined to sell the eccentric and uncomfortable palace on which her uncle, George IV. had spent so many hundreds of thousands of pounds, and seek for a seaside residence elsewhere.

It was during her first visit to Scotland in August and in September, 1842, that the Queen first really knew the pleasure of walking. Her delight when taking strolls, with only a lady in attendance, about the grounds of Dalkeith was only exceeded by the pleasure she had during her stay in Edinburgh in rising very early before the business and pleasure of the day began, and quietly visiting such points of interest as the capital of her Scottish kingdom boasted. During that stay in the North, the Queen honoured Scone and Taymouth, and did an immense deal of walking.

It was while walking on the banks of the Tay with the Duchess of Norfolk, and nothing but a distant couple of the Highland Guard to mark her rank, that the young Queen went into a cottage by the roadside. The housewife cut the ladies a few flowers, in return for which the Duchess gave her some money, saying : " From Her Majesty." At first the old dame was vastly astonished, but, at length, warmly blessed the Queen for coming to see her subjects in Scotland, thus showing more sense than many simple folk, on whom it has sometimes pleased the Queen to drop in, and who afterwards have declined to believe in the identity of their august visitor.

At Taymouth, the Queen first cultivated a taste for those unsophisticated " scrambles " which she afterwards so often made from Balmoral.

Two years later, Blair Castle was lent to the Queen by Lord Glenlyon, and Her Majesty had a delightful holiday there. She thought nothing of a two hours' walk over mountain paths, or tramping through the cornfields like a daughter of the soil. One of her very favourite walks was to the Upper Falls of Bruar. The scenery there is finer now than in 1844, as the trees have grown considerably since then. The chief amusement of the Royal party was to throw stones from the overhanging height into the boiling Falls below.

It was from Blair that the Queen first went out deerstalking with Prince Albert. Until the day of his death Her Majesty always accompanied the Prince Consort on these expeditions, frequently over most dangerous ground and sometimes in fearful weather. Particularly was this the case when the whole party went out shooting among the hills above Dhu Loch. The wind was terrific and the road almost impassable, the fords were full, and the Glassalt in particular gave the Queen some trouble to scramble over. Until the Queen herself improved the path to her favourite retreat of Alt-na-Guithasach, it was quite terrible, yet Her Majesty walked it pluckily.

It was while the Queen was out on one of the expeditions to Dhu Loch that a gillie, named Mackenzie, followed her with a letter from Lord Derby announcing the death of the Duke of Wellington. Her Majesty was almost heartbroken at her own and the nation's loss, and, amid a heavy shower, returned home at once to pen letters of condolence and comfort.

When a cairn, of which there are so many around Balmoral, was in building, the Queen would always walk, with her household and gillies, to the chosen spot, and not unfrequently insist upon carrying the stone herself.

The Scotch servants and keepers dearly liked the Queen to accompany any expedition, shooting or otherwise. They always said that things went well when she was present. "It's Her Majesty's coming that has brought good luck," and " Her Majesty has a lucky foot," were quite sayings among them.

In these modern days, when women copy the costumes of men for all sporting purposes, or when engaged in heavy walking and climbing, it says much for the Queen's stamina and courage, that she undertook such laborious exercise when trammelled with the cumbersome garments in vogue during the '40's and '50's. For at that time the only concession made to comfort or safety in walking was a slight looping up of the dress skirt over the many voluminous petticoats.

But all the Queen's walks were not of so trying a nature as when she was following the guns in the Highlands. At Windsor the walks were many and beautiful, and comprised every yard of the Home Park, the Frogmore Gardens, and those fairy glades on the north side of the Castle, known as the Slopes. A very favourite walk which the Queen, with her husband, children, and Court, used to take after service on Sunday morning, included a visit to the stables and a stroll through the Home Park to the Shaw Farm. On Sunday afternoons Her Majesty, with the Court, used to walk on the East and North Terraces, literally among her people. For all were allowed to enter the Royal gardens and crowd round their beloved Sovereign, who moved among her subjects absolutely unguarded, and with only a few gentlemen of the Court to make a clear way for her to pass. Nowadays the scene at Windsor is practically the same, save that the gracious central figure takes no part in the action. Her Majesty now sits in the *loggia* at the head of the splendid double Italian staircase that adorns the east front of her Castle, and with benevolent eyes and kindly smile surveys her people flocking to the exquisite gardens and terraces, just as they did when she herself moved so freely and unostentatiously among them.

Through the thickly planted walks and drives on the "Slopes," the Queen used to attain the "Rosary" and "The Grottoes," and also what remained of the noble tree that tradition has named "Herne's Oak." This tree was blown down some years ago, but the Queen, faithful to the past, has planted another oak on the identical spot.

The "Rosary" is a charming little oval-shaped inclosure, hedged closely round with evergreens, and having a mass of very fine rhododendron plants in the centre. A path all round it leads to the Queen's summer-house, a cosy retreat, thatched inside and out with straw. A little farther on is the ice skating rink. It is shallow, lined with asphalte, and can easily be flooded and frozen. The late Prince Henry of Battenberg used it daily during the wintry weather, he being a magnificent skater. It was made by order of the Queen, after the occasion when the late Prince Consort was nearly drowned one day skating, and when Her Majesty was herself instrumental in saving his life.

When walking from the "Rosary" to the "Grottoes," the Queen passed below the East Terrace. Here on the right is a charming model of "'Dacko,' the favourite Dachshund of the Queen. Born February, 1859; died December, 1871." On the left is a statue of "Noble," a very pet dog, whose greatest pleasure was to guard his Royal mistress's gloves. He is here represented with one of them in his charge. The Prince Consort's favourite hound, "Eos," aged 10, is also memorialised near the same spot.

The Grottoes are quaintly cut into the heart of a great chalk rock, which in formation is like a disused pit, and now has a zig-zag shaped artificial lake for fish in the centre. The grottoes are all faced with pebbles and buttressed with flints. The largest of them, which is semi-circular and runs in winding fashion far into the rock, has a small skylight above and is said to have a deep well beneath it. It is icily cool in the hottest weather. Tradition states that these grottoes were once prisons, and were connected with "Underground Windsor" by a secret passage.

Other picturesque features of the Slopes are a babbling brook (which is crossed by a most beautiful walk of lime trees that leads to Datchet), and the wonderful animal life that abounds there. Hares, rabbits, squirrels, and sleek brown rats play and gambol all day long among the old trees, which in winter offer a strange spectacle, covered, as they are, with mistletoe.

It is through these ideally sylvan surroundings that the Queen once walked so frequently, and that she now drives to the Castle whenever she reaches Windsor by the South-Western Railway.

The prettiest scenes in the Queen's life must, however, have been her many evening walks, to which she was very partial in fair, warm weather. One of these walks, which gave the Queen great pleasure and amusement, was taken after a great banquet in Trinity Hall, Cambridge, followed by a reception in honour of the Prince Consort's installation as Chancellor of the University. After the entertainments were over, the Queen proposed to walk out before retiring for the night. It was about ten o'clock when she and the Court set out in " curious costume " as Her Majesty herself says, " Albert in his dress coat with a mackintosh over it. I, in my evening dress and diadem, with a veil over my head ; the two Princes in their uniform, and the ladies in their (evening) dresses and shawls and veils."

In this strange guise did the Queen and her party first lose their way in the dark, then find the right road that led them through the avenues of lime trees in the grounds of St. John's, down to the water and over the bridges. Could any expedition be more *naïve* and simple?

A grander scene occurred once on the exquisite East Terrace at Windsor, by the light of a full, August moon. The Queen had been having a great dinner party, and afterwards led the way in all the glory of her evening gown and glittering jewels round the Terrace, while her guests and suite followed her. Every one was in full dress or uniform. The Castle lit up in every window made a fitting background to so picturesque a spectacle.

Such brilliant scenes form no part nowadays in the Queen's retired life, but they must remain a happy memory, even as to her subjects they must ever be of interest.

CHAPTER XIII

THE QUEEN AS A HOUSEKEEPER

BEFORE going any farther into descriptions of the places which give colour to the home life of Her Majesty, it may be well to say something general about the Queen as a Housekeeper, so that the reader may the better understand such intimate details of her life as it is my business and my pleasure to describe.

As we go along my readers will gather that the Queen is an exceedingly homely and hard working woman, and very far removed from the typical royal personage who is supposed to sit on a golden throne, with no thoughts, and nothing to do but to sign her name to death warrants and Acts of Parliament, or to dub mayors "knights" with a tailor's sword.

Indeed, there is nothing which goes on of which she has not intimate knowledge and which she does not shape and colour with her hand and individuality.

Fifty anecdotes will go to show this later on, but one at least may be introduced here which seems peculiarly appropriate to the heading of this chapter. Some years ago the German Ambassador had the honour of an invitation to Windsor. During an audience with Her Majesty the small talk led round to Germany and to Fürstenburg, the place of his birth. That evening at dinner, to the intense surprise of everybody familiar with the services usually in use at Her Majesty's table, the plates were of a totally different pattern and colour from the ordinary gold, silver, or blue service, of which we shall hear more farther on. On examination, the service proved to be one made at a great china factory at Fürstenburg, and each plate contained a different view of that town and neighbourhood. Though this service had not been used for nine years, and might not unnaturally have been supposed to have been broken, disposed of, or anywhere but at Windsor, Her Majesty not only recalled it, but remembered where it was, and, as a delicate compliment, had ordered it to be used at table that night.

This, if read aright, will give the reader some idea of Her Majesty's qualities as a housekeeper, and I may go so far as to say there never was any article, however insignificant or in whatever department, which has ever entered into Her Majesty's life of which she does not retain an absolute remembrance and knowledge, while those about her will tell you that no one ever knows when she will ask for something of which every one else has forgotten the existence and the whereabouts.

In her early married life her household gave her grave dissatisfaction owing to the lack of order and discipline and to the great waste of time and money. The Baroness Lehzen, who had been her governess, had become her private secretary, and had taken unto herself the management of her Royal mistress' domestic duties, and was not at all inclined to surrender them to Her Majesty or the Prince Consort ; while the Lord Steward, the Lord Chamberlain, and the Master of the Horse—all heads of various domestic departments—were equally unwilling to submit to any control. The internal arrangements at both

Buckingham Palace and Windsor were in such a state of chaos that Prince Albert, in despair, wrote to Prince von Lowenstein :—

"In my home life I am very happy and contented ; but the difficulty in filling my place with the proper dignity is that I am only the husband and not the master of the house."

To such a pitch of confusion, discomfort, and delay did matters arrive that the ever-confided-in Baron Stockmar, always ready to smooth the creases from royal rose-leaves, drew up a memorandum in which he rather humorously described the duties of the Royal Steward as being to provide and lay the fuel which the Lord Chamberlain lighted ; to supply the lamps, needles, wicks, and oil which the Lord Chamberlain cleaned, lit, trimmed, and stuffed ; and he went on to show that amid so many masters the male and female servants came on and off duty at their own bidding, and remained absent for hours and hours for the want of any one to correct their irregularities and excuses, all of which was to the detriment of convenience, cleanliness, and security.   To such a length did the irregularities of red-tape run, that a young chimney-sweep, "the boy Jones," as he was called, was several times found, like Tom in the "Water Babies," hiding in the Queen's apartments.   Indeed, there was far more in the "Bedchamber Question" than apparently Sir Robert Peel ever understood or explained.   However, in 1844, matters righted themselves so far that the heads of departments and all subordinates came under the authority of the Master of the Household.

But even this arrangement has never made Her Majesty relinquish her prerogative with regard to her servants and the internal economy of her house, and so satisfactory has been her supervision, that even when, in early days, she gave large and expensive fêtes and banquets to Emperors and Kings, there was always money with which to pay the piper.

It seems somewhat strange, but certainly to his credit, that Sir Robert Peel should have acknowledged this in such gracious words when referring to the visits of the Emperor Nicholas of Russia and King Louis Philippe:

"Those visits, of necessity, created a considerable increase of expenditure, but through that wise system of economy which is the only source of true magnificence, Her Majesty was able to meet every charge and to give a reception to the Sovereigns which struck every one by its magnificence without adding one tittle to the burdens of the country. I am not required by Her Majesty to press for the extra expenditure of one single shilling on account of these unforeseen causes of increased expenditure. I think that to state this is only due to the personal credit of Her Majesty, who insists upon it, that there shall be every magnificence required by her station, but without incurring one single debt."

Throughout her career this policy of splendid economy has been preserved, and everything is paid for as punctually as if Her Majesty had no credit and had to pay ready money for all she buys. Some idea of the size of the household over which she presides may be gathered from the fact that, not taking into account Buckingham Palace, Balmoral Castle, and Osborne House, Windsor Castle alone is a small town. It shelters and gives employment to some two thousand persons, and it may interest readers to know that during Her Majesty's absence from any of her palaces, the servants are placed on board wages, and during her flying visits to London their meals are duly catered for.

Her Majesty's household duties commence early in the

morning, when at breakfast are submitted to her certain suggestions from the clerk of the kitchen, from which she orders the dinner of the day, also selecting the meals for those of her young grandchildren who may be with her. Her alteration of the menus to be provided are made with her own hand, generally in violet ink-pencil, and are thus sent back to the kitchens, confectionery, and other departments, before ten o'clock, to be carried out. What these menus contain and what Her Majesty eats and drinks will form chapters to themselves, but in passing it may be as well to state that the stores are ordered from day to day, and her tradespeople are equally divided all over the kingdom, many articles of food and household use coming from Scotland and London when she is at Windsor, and quite as many being sent to Scotland or Osborne from London, the beech log firing (to give the first instance to hand), being sent by water from Marlow-on-Thames.

Though the locks and keys of Windsor Castle are almost all uniform (the master key being stamped with the name of "Hobbs and Co.," "If found, 20s. reward," initials and a number which it would be indiscreet to give), all the servants have, as I have said, their allotted regions, beyond the limits of which they are not permitted to stray. Under Her Majesty's *régime* everything appertaining to her household has its number, place, and season. The huge bee-hive moves in perfect order and concord, knowing by instinct and by example that though kindness and every consideration are shown to everybody, no one is sufficiently valuable to be indispensable, and that backsliding will not be permitted, and that even the most elementary things are noticed and heard of, as also that the work is, except at moments, light and well paid. There is no mistress so kind as the Queen, for she hates new faces, and not only never parts with a good servant, but, even when they grow

THE ROYAL NURSERIES.

old or are incapacitated by sickness, she pensions them off
in some snug house where they have little or nothing to
do, and are well paid and looked after, with plenty of
good food and firing, and a doctor specially retained to
administer to their wants.

Every single article of linen, blankets, bedding, carpets,
curtains, and furniture is numbered and catalogued, and
is continually checked and reported on, and in its turn
is either washed, re-picked, beaten, cleaned, or polished,
according to its class.   The Queen is very particular as to
any form of dirt or even untidiness, and there is a story
told of Her Majesty having come across a neglected
cabinet in one of the unoccupied little suites off the Grand
Corridor, and writing her well-known signature with her
finger in the dust.   Going the next day to see the result of
this silent rebuke, she found that no notice had been taken
of it, and accordingly wrote the name of the particular
housemaid who was responsible for the neglect under-
neath.   The next day the two signatures had disappeared,
and so had the housemaid, who was so frightened that
she ran away without even asking for a character.   The
Queen, however, sent for her, had her brought back, and
spoke to her kindly.

Yet even queens are not always infallible.   On one
occasion—some few years after her marriage—Buckingham
Palace and all the State departments were thrown into a
condition of intense excitement.   The Queen, on returning
from her ride, missed her keys, and whether they had been
dropped by Her Majesty in the Palace or out of doors no
one could tell.   For hours the Palace was in a ferment,
even the Queen joining in the search for the lost keys,
while the question of altering the locks of all the despatch-
boxes, safes, and various private receptacles belonging to
the Queen herself was seriously mooted.   The great expense

that such a proceeding would entail was finally obviated by
the recovery of the keys. The Queen, though much worried
at the time by the occurrence, has often since told the story
against herself.

CHAPTER XIV

THE QUEEN AND HER STORE-ROOMS

TO attempt to depict the inner life of the great lady who rules our land, to shadow forth her haunts and habits, her temperament and characteristics, and to omit all mention of her linen-room, store-cupboard, and the spots where her glass and china find resting place, were to render this record woefully incomplete.

For it is to the orderly rules of the Queen, and indirectly to the late Prince Consort, that neatness and method have been evolved out of the extravagance, waste, and untidiness which prevailed in the Royal Palaces on Her Majesty's accession sixty years ago.

At that time things that were perhaps of but little worth individually, though valuable in the mass, were made away with wholesale. The perquisite system was in full force, and wine or candles, and other imperishable articles which had been produced for any particular occasion and had remained untouched, were calmly annexed by certain officials and their underlings, although perfectly fit to be brought forth again. Those were the days when scores of people outside the palaces lived in luxury on the proceeds of robbery and waste within.

It was all this, as well as the various cliques that supported the system, that the young husband and wife—themselves little more than children—had to combat, and it is from that disorder that the delightfully arranged store-rooms of the Queen have sprung.

It must first be premised that, good and domestic economist as Her Majesty has proved herself, she has never ground the faces of her tradespeople by giving them wholesale orders at reduced prices. Hence it is that the chief store-room at Windsor, although a large enough apartment, is never unduly crowded with a vast quantity of material. The room is almost lined from floor to ceiling with cupboards which are cut into pigeon holes. Each has its own little door and each contains some different article of household consumption.

A large table fills the centre of the room, a few chairs, a desk, and weights and scales complete the equipment of this very plain apartment. Here come every day the various menus for the Queen's luncheon and dinner and for the meals served in the Royal nurseries. The menus have already passed through the Queen's hands—it cannot be too strongly impressed on indolent housewives and frivolous girls that Her Majesty practically orders all the meals served to her—and arrive in the store-room with the quantities of materials required for each dish duly annotated against it by the kitchen authorities. Other menus, those to be served to the Household, the Equerries' breakfast, even the meals for the servants, are all obliged to go through the same process of superintendence by clerks of the kitchen and store-rooms and of head cooks. The mornings are spent in the store-rooms by giving out what is required, stating this in a series of books, and in seeing what stores need replenishment.

It should be noted that no fish, meat, vegetables, butter, or other perishable articles ever come into this store-room.

In fact their nature prevents them from being looked upon in the light of stores. The materials which are used in the Confectionery Kitchens are kept in a room apart from the General Stores.

This is an apartment leading from the principal confectionery kitchen. It is all snow-white and fitted everywhere with small cupboards and glass-covered receptacles for every kind of material used in fine confectionery. In the centre of the room is a great glass case containing specimens of the Chief Confectioner's skill.

It is in this room that all the cakes and sweets made for the Queen are checked according to the order book and packed for despatch to whatever place the Court may be. A list of the dainties sent to Her Majesty at Balmoral on September 1st, 1892, may be interesting to those who share their Sovereign's weakness of a " sweet tooth."

1 Box of Biscuits.
1 Box Drop Tablets.
1 Box of Pralines.
16 Chocolate Sponges.
12 Plain Sponges.
16 Fondant Biscuits.
1 Box of Wafers, containing 2 or 3 dozen of Fancy Shapes.
1½ dozen Flat Finger Biscuits.
1 Sponge Cake.
1 Princess Cake.
1 Rice Cake.

This order, which with sundry varieties is expected three or four times a week, is always addressed thus :

"This package to be delivered at the Equerries' Entrance at Buckingham Palace."

From thence the Queen's Messenger conveys it to the Court.

There are two fine linen-rooms at Windsor Castle. All linen used by the Queen is of the finest and best, the table linen being really magnificent. Many of the designs are repetitions of those used fifty or sixty years ago, and in most the insignia of the Garter, the Royal Arms, or the national emblems of Great Britain appear. All the linen used in the Palaces is gone through every year with the greatest care, and every piece that shows even the faintest sign of wear is put aside for presentation to hospitals and charitable institutions as "cast linen." It is a very vulgar error to believe, as many people do, that the "cast linen" given away by the Queen is body linen.

More interesting than the linen-rooms is the big "China and Glass Room," which is approached through the principal store-room. So charmingly arranged is this large, bright apartment that the first view of it is like that of a very well-set-out shop. Wide shelves line the white walls, one set of which is inclosed by glass doors. It is to the topmost shelf of all that the eye is first attracted, by the line of large flower-pots of fine jasper Wedgwood ware. They are modern and were made expressly for use at the wedding-breakfast of Princess Beatrice and the late Prince Henry of Battenberg, which took place at Osborne.

Of dinner services there is a great variety. Many of them are very valuable and of marvellous beauty, others again are merely quaint. But all seem superfluous where the meals are almost always served on solid gold and silver.

The prettiest china is a full service of French (Chantilly) ware. The borders of each piece are of Royal blue and rich gold, and the centre of exquisitely painted birds. The plates are valued at ten guineas each. A Dresden service is also extremely beautiful, being of a very elegant design and most delicate in colouring. A Worcester Harlequin Service is handsome, but very bizarre in effect, and it is not surprising to hear that it is never used at the Queen's table.

More strange is it to know that a splendid set of Chelsea ware, painted in the most brilliant and characteristic manner with birds and butterflies, is also seldom now taken from the store-room. A china maniac would give any sum for such wonderful ware. A Sèvres Service for dinner and dessert is green in its general colouring. It sometimes makes an appearance in the Household Dining-room, and sometimes the Queen uses the dessert plates.

The only china service, however, that finds favour in Her Majesty's eyes is a very pretty one that was made for her by Minton eighteen years ago. It has a beautiful blue border, with medallions inclosing the rose, shamrock, and thistle, painted in the Sèvres style. The centre of each piece is filled by a blue medallion, on which are the entwined letters V.R. in thickly raised gold. This service, which is very large, and includes a number of splendid fruit dishes, is always used on great occasions, such as the Duke of York's wedding, the visits of the German Emperor to Cowes, and the Tsar to Balmoral. It was also in constant use during all the grand Jubilee festivities. It is a noteworthy fact that only one plate has been broken during the years it has been used.

An Etruscan service in black and red ware is peculiarly ugly and heavy, and, with a service of Fürstenberg ware which is very beautifully painted with landscapes, brings the list of the Queen's dinner services to a close.

Of coffee and tea sets the Queen has a multitude. The most charming is of fine Sèvres, having a wine-coloured ground, panelled with exquisite landscapes and heads in medallions. A Burmese tea service of twelve pieces is of a most peculiar waxen tint which shades to pink at the edges. It is elaborately decorated in a raised gold design. Princess

Beatrice frequently uses it, but its fragility is extreme, and it is only fit for a cabinet specimen.

One particular table is set apart in the China room for all the quaint odds and ends that were given to the Queen in her childhood and to her own children.   Here are Stafford-shire figures, Cottage ware, queer pieces of Lustre, and above all a wonderful pair of spotted dogs, the like of which for quaintness and hideousness could not be matched through-out the length and breadth of Her Majesty's kingdom.

The glass used for ordinary occasions at the Queen's table is extremely thin and light, but severely simple in shape, and merely decorated on one side with Her Majesty's cipher.

On State occasions the magnificent old cut-glass is brought out.   This is of the finest workmanship, and great weight, while its price is almost incalculable, as every year that passes adds much to its value.   The same system of giving out china and glass prevails in the store-room of these articles as in the Gold and Silver Pantries.

Yet with all the care and system which prevails in the Queen's Palaces, articles sometimes go astray in an un-accountable fashion.   On one occasion the late Prince Henry of Battenberg sent to the Land and Water Exhibition a picture of his favourite hunter.   After a time the Prince asked that his picture should be returned to him on the following day, and a messenger was duly sent from Windsor to London to receive the painting.   For days the picture was lost, but at length it reached Osborne, having been sent there by mistake from Buckingham Palace.   The Royal Family were not a little astonished to find that such an error could have been made.

CHAPTER XV

WHAT THE QUEEN READS

THAT the Queen has all her life been an omnivorous reader can be readily understood by all who appreciate the broadness of her views, and her sympathetic knowledge of things and men, more especially of such as are touched by the sorrows of this world. No class of literature that is faintly worthy has been neglected by Her Majesty, and her memory, which is truly extraordinary, has always assisted her in the practical understanding of what she reads. As a child and young person she had a great love of history, and devoured everything that had to do with the making of England and the lives of those who had occupied the throne. On a question of dates or sequence of historical events the Queen's memory is to this day unrivalled. While her just and impartial criticism of even the salt of the earth was once exemplified during a conversation she had with Macaulay shortly after reading his history, when she said : " I am afraid I cannot say much for my ancestor, James II."

" Your Majesty's predecessor, not ancestor," cried the historian.

The Queen laughingly acknowledged the compliment, but did not change her opinion about the deposed monarch.

Dean Stanley, during his long and intimate friendship with the Queen, frequently referred his printed works to her judgment and discretion, and it was in his drawing-room that Her Majesty met Carlyle. The sage of Chelsea was not at all abashed by being in his Sovereign's presence, and, pulling up a chair quite close to her, proceeded in his quaint way to cross-question her on her historical knowledge, likes, and dislikes. He acknowledged to being much impressed by the terseness and sense of her remarks, which, he maintained, contrasted agreeably with the rambling inaccuracies of the majority of women.

To the meanest observer it must be evident that the reading got through by the Queen each day is enormous. Her vast private correspondence, the Parliamentary reports from the hand of the Leader of the House of Commons, despatches from every Government office, and duly-considered excerpts from the leading daily papers are all read by or to the Queen by her private secretary, maid-of-honour, and lady-in-waiting, and are considered by the Queen in the light of business. Books that are read for ˏinstruction or amusement are taken later in the day, and of these Her Majesty generally has three or four going at a time, preferring to sandwich memoirs and travels with novels and the contents of the more evanescent magazine. Even when her arduous day is done, and at one o'clock in the morning the Queen betakes herself to bed, the lady-in-waiting reads to Her Majesty until the signal comes for extinguishing all the lights but the *veilleuse*.

The post of " Reader to the Queen " is a charming appointment, and accompanied with much interest. Miss Heath, the handsome young actress, who afterwards became Mrs. Wilson Barrett, held the office for years, and frequently travelled to Windsor to fulfil her duties. Shakespeare's plays and the Queen's favourite poets were always laid under contributions on such occasions, for Her Majesty, who has a singularly true and keen ear for cadence and correct emphasis, never can bear to hear verse delivered by any but the most carefully trained voice. Miss Glynn was another gifted elocutionist who was for many years "Reader to the Queen." At the same time it must be understood that all the ladies about the Court must be able to read with just expression and clear accent. Princess Beatrice is a most beautiful reader, and the art is one which the Queen had carefully inculcated in all her children.

And now it will be interesting to show what are the particular books that have ever been dear as friends to the Queen, and where and how the splendid collections of literary curiosities, that are a great feature of Windsor, are housed. Appropriately the library is arranged in one of the oldest portions of the Castle, being that wing that Queen Elizabeth added to the Royal residence for her own private use. A quaintly shaped *E* in iron still hangs on the south wall of the library, while the north side is pierced by a grand window, set in carved stone mullions, and overlooking the copses that flourish beneath the North Walk, the "Hundred Steps," Eton, and the river meads.

The interior of this wing, which was once cut up into small rooms, was altered by William IV.'s favourite architect, Sir Jeffry Wyattville, and made into a most noble apartment, of which the chief historical interest is concentrated at the further end. Here is the wonderful fireplace and stone mantel built by Elizabeth, and bearing her bust and the date 1583. Its intrinsic beauty is great, and its interest unparalleled, as it is the most handsome and characteristic piece of Elizabethan decoration in the country. Nearly opposite is the famous Blenheim Room. This is a very small polygonal chamber, built in the turret above an old Norman Gateway. It was once the bay of

Henry VII.'s private room, and contracted though it is—there is only space within it for a couple of armchairs—was used by Queen Anne as a boudoir. Here was she sitting when news of the battle of Blenheim was brought her, and here for many years were hung the flags which the Dukes of Marlborough presented to the Sovereign on every anniversary of the great battle. The view from this chamber is the most beautiful of any at Windsor, and Prince Albert used to—and nowadays the Empress Frederick does—sit there to read. The painted ceiling was raised by the Prince Consort, and decorated from his design. He also had a great deal to do with the present arrangement of the library.

The furniture is of ebony and scarlet leather, and an immense number of large armchairs are on every side. Down the centre of the library, which is over eighty feet long, are glass-topped tables of ebony, inlaid with ivory. In them may be found the priceless nucleus of the collection, the famous Mentz Psalter of 1457, which was given to George III. by the University of Gottingen, and of which only two other copies exist, one in Vienna, and the other in Berlin (this volume was printed in colours long before Caxton's time, and is valued at £10,000); the vellum Caxton, the rare Aldine Virgil of 1505, the copy of Shakespeare of 1632, which Charles I. autographed and gave to Sir Thomas Herbert just before his execution, many missals of exquisite beauty that have belonged to England's former Queens, and the manuscript copy of Shah Jehan, an extraordinary illuminated Persian work, which, however, is scarcely more interesting than the illustrated Abyssinian Bible that once belonged to King Theodore. Of Eastern books and rare Latin and Greek folios there are also a goodly number, the majority of them having been " retained " for himself by George IV. when in a fit of economy he turned out the

Royal Library from Buckingham Palace in 1823, and "presented" the sixty-five thousand choice volumes to the British Museum, where it is now known as the "King's Library."

Other treasures beneath glass are Queen Elizabeth's prayer-book, a facsimile of the pencil letter from the Duke of Marlborough to his wife Sarah, written on the field of Blenheim, a letter from that good Bishop Juxon, who accompanied Charles I. to the scaffold, and the last ticket ever used by the Prince Consort at the last Eton montem but one.

Also under glass is the wonderful orrery of Sir Walter Scott, and a letter explaining its movements, and William IV.'s silver microscope.

It will take many years before such a fine collection of books will be gathered together at Windsor as George IV. disposed of, though the works so carefully arranged in the different departments of topography, art, genealogy, history, reference, general knowledge, poetry, and fiction, have been steadily growing in numbers since the beginning of the Queen's reign, the whole being under the care of a Chief Librarian who has apartments in the Castle and an assistant, while yet another expert looks after the treasures of the adjoining Print Room.

A very great many of the Queen's books are in the Reference department bound in vellum, but books of general interest and which are in constant request are left in their original covers. And it is in those works which are almost in daily use that most interest will be taken by those who would wish to know what the Queen reads and what she has read. Almost first in Her Majesty's favour come the works of Scott, those she likes most being "The Antiquary," "The Talisman," and "Peveril of the Peak." Of his poems she is extremely fond, and she possesses a copy of them with his own emendations of them on the margin, while her love of Scotland has frequently been expressed by her to her friends in apt quotations from " The Lady of the Lake," " Marmion," and the " Lay of the Last Minstrel." The Queen's admiration for Scott's works has induced her to have one room at Balmoral entirely decorated with scenes from his poems and books. Jane Austen's novels have also been very popular with the Queen. A few of Lord Beaconsfield's works are here, and a handsome copy of " Lothair," in three volumes and bound in royal blue, contains the inscription : " For the Queen from a faithful servant ;" Kingsley's " Saints' Tragedy," and " Two Years Ago," Tennyson's " Idylls of the King," Trollope's " Barchester Towers," a complete set of Thackeray's works, some of the Brontés' and Edna Lyall's books, many of R. L. Stevenson's romances, Rudyard Kipling's stories, Edmund Yates' " Reminiscences," and nearly all Mrs. Oliphant's novels ; Rider Haggard's " She," " Jess," and " Handley Cross ;" Sponge's " Sporting Tour," and two full editions of Dickens' books—one, a library edition ; the other the last published *Edition de Luxe*—are all conspicuous on these characteristically filled shelves. The Queen also possesses and values greatly an original unpublished manuscript of Charles Dickens.

About Dickens and the Queen there is a most touching little story which the passage of time makes it possible to relate. ¡The great author, while still early in his career, conceived the most passionate attachment for Her Majesty, the girlish beauty which she retained unimpaired for very many years after her marriage, and her sweet grace having made the deepest impression on Dickens. He went everywhere he was likely to be able to see her, and in a most touching letter to Mr. Thompson, then a light in literary circles, and the father of Mrs. Alice Meynell, and the well-known artist Lady Butler, he poured out his love for the Queen, not as his Sovereign, but as a woman. In this same letter he described how he had spent days and weeks in the neighbourhood of Windsor, hiding among the trees in the Park and lounging about her favourite drives so that he might sometimes catch a glimpse of her. The Queen once saw Dickens act at a charity performance, and one of her pet Skye-terriers was named " Boz."

Among other books which the Queen keeps in the drawing-room at Osborne and her private drawing-room at Balmoral are " The Vicar of Wakefield," in French, " Pen-and-Ink-Notes," " Mountain, Loch, and Glen," and editions of Scott, Dickens, the Brontés, and other standard writers of fiction.

It must not be thought, however, that the reading of the Queen and her Court is restricted by the limits of the Royal Library. Large boxes of current literature in English, French, and German follow Her Majesty from Mudie's wherever she may be, and all the Court have access to them. But the Queen has many favourites also that she takes everywhere, and six huge cases of books from the library are an invariable item in the Royal baggage. Besides this, when the Queen is away from Windsor, works touching on State business, maps, or indexes are frequently telegraphed for or fetched by the messenger who travels daily between Windsor and wherever the Queen may be.

It is only like the Queen's desire for others' happiness that the Library is always free to those about her, who are also allowed to have books in their own rooms. Etiquette demands, however, that when one of the Royal family is using the Library, every one should absent himself save the persons in attendance and the librarian.

In these later years the Queen is debarred from visiting her Library in person as it is only accessible by a narrow winding staircase rising from one corner of the Print Room. But Her Majesty is a constant visitor to the Print Room, which she enters by a door which leads into the private apartments of the Prince Consort. Above this door is a black medallion portrait of the late Prince and an inscription.

The Print Room, in which is stored the most valuable collection of prints in the world, is lined throughout with oak cases, in which are arranged in proper order the priceless contents. The whole centre of the room is filled with a very large table, at which the Queen delights to sit and look through these treasures. The spaces between and opposite the windows are also filled with low sets of oak shelves, the tops of which are crowded with many interesting and rare relics. The most delightful of all of these is a little water-colour sketch executed by the Queen of herself when she was only ten years old, and presented by her to George IV. on his last birthday. It bears the date August 12th, 1829.

Three small coloured sketches near by belonged to Charles I. A most quaint relic which Her Majesty values very much is a small full-length water-colour of the great Napoleon, taken six weeks before his death, in the identical clothes in which he was afterwards buried. An inscription on the back shows that the picture was given to a former Lord Londonderry, who presented it to his secretary, Mr. R. Wood. Through Mr. Wood it came into the possession of the Honourable Mary Hughes, a maid of honour, from whom the Queen was graciously pleased to accept it on March 13, 1893.

Linley Sambourne's original sketch of Sir Henry Thompson, which was drawn for *Punch*, hangs in the Print Room, the fairest adornment of which, however, is a copy of the famous bust at Bonn, by which Lili, the celebrated modeller, has immortalised in coloured wax the perfect features of Raphael's favourite model. This is most appropriate in a room where the most famous collection of Raphael's prints reposes.

It is in this shrine of art that the Queen and her daughters spend much of their time, and here that Mr. Holmes, the librarian, keeps his interesting record of the works that pass from his hand to those of the Queen.

But the three favourite books of Her Majesty do not ever leave her intimate company. Her Bible, with the Book of Common Prayer, and a volume of Hymns Ancient and Modern, in their simple binding, are always by her side. Much of her fortitude under suffering and the consolations for her afflictions have been drawn from these sources, and among books that the Queen reads they should have important mention.

CHAPTER XVI

THE QUEEN AS A DANCER

ENDOWED as the Queen has always been with perfectly healthy instincts, and taking infinite pleasure in all forms of exercise and innocent recreation, one of her favourite forms of amusement has been dancing. Herself a very beautiful and graceful performer of every kind of dance, she is still most critical on the subject, and though since the death of the Prince Consort Her Majesty has never attended any function where dancing is in progress, all her grandchildren in turn have been through their steps before her and been duly corrected as to deportment and carriage, while nothing pleases her so much as to see a minuet or some other old-world measure danced in the course of a play.

But that the Queen's likings are not bound by tradition is shown by the fact that she is a great appreciator of skirt-dancing as rendered by the younger members of her Court, and there is an excellent story told of the pleasure Her Majesty took in a very pretty dance that the Hon. Mary Lambert, a maid of honour, performed for the amusement of her Royal mistress one evening. After much applause and praise, the Queen asked Miss Lambert what gift she should bestow on her for dancing so well. The smart reply was : " The head of Mr. —— in a charger."

In the Queen's childish days, when she was kept as much as possible from Court, she was frequently taken to the Opera, which in those times always included a ballet. How much the young Princess was impressed with these displays of dancing is shown by the fact that she dressed and named many of her dolls after the best-known dancers of the period. The great Taglioni and her sisters, that lovely Duvernay whom Thackeray worshipped and the banker Lyne-Stephens married, Brocard, Leontine Heberte, the Sisters Aucilin, Leconte, and the ballet master Albert, were all represented again and again in different characters by the patient fingers of the Princess and her governess.

The Princess danced but little, however, at balls before her accession ; but when, after her marriage, she began her happy home life, small dances at Buckingham Palace and Windsor were of very frequent occurrence. At Windsor the *venue* chosen for these quite informal evenings was always the Crimson Drawing-room, the largest of the three beautiful private reception-rooms that overlook the famous East Terrace. The floor, which is of satin and tulip woods, was always kept in the most exquisite order for dancing. A fine grand piano frequently sufficed as music, though sometimes a small recessed room was used for a band. Here, on the crimson silk-panelled walls, hang portraits of the Duke and Duchess of Kent. The six cabinets and a beautiful pair of Amboyna wood tables, inlaid with mother-of-pearl and tortoiseshell, along with a huge vase of polished granite which Alexander II. sent the Queen from Russia, are the principal features of an apartment which still wears much the same appearance as at the beginning of the Queen's reign.

Frequently the Queen would suggest a little dance among the Court, and much fun was often caused by the paucity of ladies on these occasions. In 1842, when a party was

assembled at Windsor in honour of the Prince of Wales'
christening, dancing was started one evening for the amusement of young Prince Leopold of Saxe-Coburg. There
were only enough ladies present to make up a quadrille,
which the Queen danced with the King (afterwards the first
Emperor) of Prussia. The evening wound up with a gay
country dance, a form of exercise to which the Queen was
devoted. She learnt from old books every kind of figure,
and, however obsolete, always studied them herself and
taught them to her ladies.

The evenings at Frogmore, where the Queen, Prince
Albert, and a few members of the Court frequently visited
the Duchess of Kent, after dinner often ended in a regular
romp, one very favourite dance being a *contre danse* called
Grandpère, which was nothing more or less than "Follow-
my-Leader," and in which every one joined with great
enthusiasm.

The dances at Buckingham Palace were never quite as
friendly as those at Windsor, but they were generally kept
very small, the Queen dancing and talking with every one.
It is noteworthy, however, that young as Her Majesty was
at the time, and full of youthful spirits, she scarcely ever
waltzed with any one but the Prince Consort or a Royal
visitor. The quadrille, then the fashionable dance, she
would bestow upon her other guests. These little parties
were never very late, for the Queen generally retired at 1.30
and the suppers were quite simple and informal.

Almost the first improvements the Queen made at
Buckingham Palace was to add the present magnificent
ballroom and at once to inaugurate a series of splendid
State balls. In 1842 she conceived the idea of giving a
grand Fancy Dress Ball, a style of fête that had died in
England with the Stuarts. This gorgeous entertainment
took place on April 12th and was one of the most brilliant

functions of the century. Several Royal ladies and friends of the Queen formed quadrilles for the occasion. The Queen and Prince Albert appeared as Edward III. and Queen Philippa. The beautiful marble group of Her Majesty and the Prince by Theed, which is now at Windsor represents them in these dresses.

The Queen was so delighted with the success of this ball that a few weeks later she gave another in which the costumes were confined to the periods of George II. and George III. During the following years she gave a ball of the Stuart period (a most lovely portrait of herself in the Stuart costume hangs in her private sitting-room at Windsor), and in 1845 a very grand *bal poudré* at which Her Majesty danced a minuet with infinite grace.

As the Queen's children began to grow old enough to prac- tise the steps their mother had taught them, nothing pleased Her Majesty more than to give dances and fancy balls on their birthdays. In 1854 a magnificent children's dance was given at Buckingham Palace, and that same year a splendid fancy ball was given for the Queen at the French Embassy. In fact, so fond was the Sovereign of dancing that when- ever she visited at any of the country houses of her subjects a big ball was always arranged for one evening of her stay. One of the finest of these was given at Chats- worth, at which it was noticed that the Queen enjoyed her- self immensely.

On the two occasions when the Queen made a State visit to France, once in 1843, when she stayed as the guest of Louis Philippe at the Chateau d'Eu, and again in 1855 when she visited Napoleon III., entertainments were given in which dancing was an important feature. It was during an evening party at the Chateau d'Eu that Her Majesty dis- played that amount of dignity which her simple manner and genial ways sometimes led people to think was

absent.   The room being warm, the Queen asked for
a glass of water, which was presently handed to her
by a lacquey.   Her Majesty declined to take the glass, and
Louis Philippe—the "Bourgeois," as he was rightly called
by the French—seeing that a breach of etiquette had
been committed, directed one of his sons to serve the
Queen.

At a ball given in 1855 at the Hotel de Ville, at which
the Queen danced with the Emperor Napoleon, Her
Majesty was much amused at hearing "God Save the
Queen" played as a polka.

The Queen first took a great fancy to Scotch reels when
she was on a visit to Taymouth Castle in 1842, when Lord
Breadalbane gave a ball in her honour, and after the
quadrille d'honneur a number of reels were danced.
Since that time thousands of reels, jigs, and other national
dances have been danced before the Queen, and have
always served their purpose in giving her great pleasure.
She is one of the few Southerners who can judge the
merits of a Highland dancing contest, and can tell the
difference between the steps which to the ordinary eye are
all alike.   Frequently when the Queen was yachting—and
she spent many days in each year on board her yacht
during her married life—she would have the sailors dance
before her, and it is characteristic of her thoroughness that
all her children should have been taught dancing in every
branch and style.

Although Her Majesty has not for thirty-six years set foot
inside a ballroom she always loves to know that those
about her can enjoy to the full the pleasures of dancing
she once so appreciated.   She has within the last few years
built a fine ballroom at Balmoral.   Nor is it so long ago
that Princess Beatrice gave a splendid county ball at
Osborne.   Nowadays, however, the tripping steps of her

little grandchildren and the graceful posing of those of the Maids of Honour who have studied the art, are sufficient reminders to the Queen of those days when she was acknowledged to be the best dancer in her kingdom.

CHAPTER XVII

WHAT THE QUEEN EATS AND DRINKS

SMALL children who are restricted in their appetites for cakes and "goodies" are very prone to look forward to that time when they shall be grown up and able to eat what they please, little understanding that with the freedom to eat and drink what one chooses the desire for high living generally goes.

This is essentially the case with the Queen. With all the *personnel* of her vast kitchens at her command, mistress of magnificent wine-cellars, and owner of miles of forcing houses where the most exquisite fruits and vegetables can be raised all the year round, Her Majesty's own table, though always laden with splendid plate and lovely flowers, is served far more simply than those of her wealthy subjects, while her own appetite, which was never at any time a very large one, is now more than usually small. This last characteristic marks out the Queen as being singular from among all her family. The Guelphs were ever very large eaters, and the four Georges, with all their sons and daughters, indulged appetites which were more than hearty. Most of the Queen's children and grandchildren too are large eaters, though almost all of them prefer plain food to the rich dishes which are put before them.

In other respects the Queen sets many people an

example of restraint and good taste. In spite of the vast resources at her command for the raising of food under artificial conditions, she never permits her own table or that of her Household to be served with anything that is out of season, though once a fruit, fish, or vegetable is in proper condition for eating, she expects it always to be available for use. For instance, the entire time that sweet chestnuts are in perfection they are served every night at the Queen's table, even though for weeks together no one touches them. In fact, quite half the eatables that appear daily at the Queen's table are things that she herself never eats, but at the same time likes to see about her and to know are there.

A very amusing and perfectly true story illustrates this trait in the Queen's character, and also serves to show how strong is her love of method and order, even in domestic affairs.

Although it is well known to all the Queen's cooks and personal servants that she never touches cold meat in any form, there is a stringent rule that the Royal side tables, at both luncheon and dinner, are to be well supplied with cold viands, among which a roast sirloin of beef and poultry invariably figure. On one occasion—never forgotten by Her Majesty's servants—at Balmoral it so chanced that a meagre half of a cold chicken was placed on the sideboard. The Queen noticed this breach of order as she entered the dining-room, and when seated at table, with a view of teaching her careless domestics a lesson, conveyed to Princess Beatrice and Lady Ely, who were with her, a hint to ask for chicken, she herself doing the same. The consternation that followed, and the subsequent lectures that ensued, may be better imagined than described, but since that time there has been no lack of cold chicken for the Royal table.

The Queen's Private Dining-room, where in her married life she used to dine frequently *tête-à-tête* with the Prince Consort, with not even a favourite Lady-in-Waiting to interrupt their intercourse, is a medium-sized room, panelled and ceiled entirely in oak, touched with gold. It is built out over the Queen's private entrance, and the mullioned windows look into the Quadrangle. Entrance is gained to it by a large pair of double doors, which face the head of the Queen's pretty white and gold staircase, and her own private apartments across the end of the Grand Corridor.

Two ample fireplaces warm the room. Above one hangs a fairly pleasing full length portrait of the Queen painted by H. von Angeli in 1877.

In order that the Queen should not be incommoded by the fires two fine screens stand before them, one being painted with birds of paradise and peacocks, and the other in three panels of flowers and shells, game and fruit, and signed H. von Pruschen, 1877. Facing the windows and above the two large oak sideboards, which with vast wine coolers beneath them flank the double doors, hang two splendid pieces of Gobelin tapestry, representing a boar hunt. They were given to the Queen by Louis Philippe. The other wall decorations in the room are portraits of the Queen's four daughters-in-law, painted in each case soon after marriage. The one of the Princess of Wales in a low, white gown and with a dark, soft ringlet hanging over either shoulder is especially pretty, and the Duchess of Edinburgh, painted in 1874 by Richter, is very handsome. Like all the Queen's private apartments the floor is covered with a rich crimson carpet in the winter, and a fine cream matting in the summer.

The service staircase, which is of stone, and very narrow and winding, leads directly down to the kitchen. The door to it is masked by a high screen of embossed leather. The following notice affixed to the wall indicates the strict order which regulates every detail of domestic service in the Queen's Palaces:

" No one is under any circumstances permitted to ascend or descend this staircase excepting those serving at or for the Royal table.
" By Order,
" The Master of the Household."

This dining-room is now used by the Queen on all possible occasions, and the lovely white and gold room in the Prince of Wales' Tower, which was re-decorated in the Jubilee year, and where so many magnificent banquets were then given, is scarcely ever used nowadays. The dining-room used by the Household, and where six to twelve sit down every day, is a very pretty little room, octagonal in shape and decorated in oak, cream, and gold. It overlooks the North Terrace, and contains a very rare old Boule clock.

Her Majesty's tastes in food are, as I have said before, most simple. A tiny slice of boiled chicken, or a cut from the sirloin, which is sent from London every day and roasted at a special fire in the kitchen, or perhaps a slice of game, which, like the beef for the Queen's use, is cooked apart, form the staple portion of Her Majesty's luncheon. She has a partiality for white soup, which in several varieties is often served to her.

The Queen's breakfasts are even plainer than her luncheons. Fish is always on the table, but eggs on toast, or merely boiled, with dry toast and a small selection of fancy bread, are the usual articles put before the Queen at her first meal. There is no doubt that Her Majesty has a strong weakness for afternoon tea. From her early days in Scotland, when Brown and the other gillies used to boil the kettle in a sheltered corner of the moors while Her

Majesty and the young Princesses sketched, the refreshing cup of tea has ever ranked high in the Royal favour.

It is principally to supply the Queen's tea-table that the confectionery cooks are kept busy all the year round at Windsor, for wherever the Court may be there must follow a large supply of cakes. Among the favourites of the Queen which are carefully packed in small tin boxes, and sent to the Court four times a week, are chocolate sponges, plain sponges, wafers of two or three different shapes, *langues de chats*, biscuits and drop cakes of all kinds, tablets, *petits fours*, princess and rice cakes, pralines, almond sweets, and a large quantity of mixed sweets.

Of all the fruit that is produced in such profusion at Frogmore the Queen prefers some highly perfumed grapes of a clear amber colour, but she is reasonably proud of the glorious pineapples and peaches that are grown for her, and frequently eats of the fine fruit the Rothschild family often send her. Among vegetables, Her Majesty confesses to a great weakness for potatoes, which are cooked for her in every conceivable way, and are—in common with all that she eats and drinks—set before her by a very faithful servant, who wears no livery, but in sober black stands by the Queen's side at her meals and assists her to everything.

That Royal appetites are subject to the vagaries that beset those of commoner folk is sometimes too true, as the officials at the Mansion House found on one occasion when the Queen and Prince Consort were partaking of the Chief Magistrate of the City's hospitality. The Queen asked for some cherry tart, and was somewhat put out when informed that there was none. Her Majesty, indeed, is very fond of all kinds of pies, and a cranberry tart with cream is one of her favourite dishes.

Of Scotch cookery the Queen has a very great appreciation, and on one occasion, when she was staying (after her widowhood) at Dunkeld with the Duke and Duchess of Athol, she was loud in her praise of the admirable table kept and most astonished to find that the cook was a Scotch woman. It was here that the Queen first tried "haggis" and liked it very much. It was also in Scotland, when staying at Dalkeith House, in 1842, that Her Majesty first ate "Finnan haddies," for in those days local delicacies did not travel far. Since then dried haddocks and oatmeal porridge are often seen at the Royal breakfast-tables. In fact, porridge and bread-and-butter frequently formed the staple food of the Queen, when in her early married life she would, with the Prince Consort and Lady Churchill, travel incognito among the small Highland towns and "put up" in small Scotch inns. On such occasions the only form of nutriment the Royal party took with them was their own wine—certainly a most necessary precaution. One dinner the Queen ate under such simple circumstances, consisted of "hotch potch" soup, which Her Majesty naïvely relates was not very much to her taste, fowl with white sauce, roast lamb, and potatoes. Another time the travellers fared very badly. The Queen, accompanied by the Prince Consort, Princess Alice, and Prince Louis of Hesse, Lady Churchill, General Grey, two maids, and three gillies, dined on tea and two starved Highland chickens without vegetables, or any kind of pudding. Yet Her Majesty kept her good nature and cheerful temper under such—for her—very trying circumstances. The Queen always had a passion for eating in the open air, and has retained her taste for so doing till the present day. On one occasion she made a delightful luncheon off warmed-up broth and potatoes she had helped to boil herself on a bitter October morning on the moors above Balmoral, while another time she greatly enjoyed a hot venison pie which the Duchess of Atholl provided for a picnic in the woods that border Loch Ordie.

But if the Ruler of the most powerful territories in the world be simple in the taste she displays in her eating, her likes in the matter of what beverages she takes are plainer still, and this in the face of the fact that her cellars at Buckingham Palace, Windsor Castle, and St. James's Palace, enjoy world-wide reputation, not only from their vast extent, but for the wonderful contents thereof. A great deal of the rare wine in the Royal cellars was laid down by George IV., who, being privileged to import wine duty free, availed himself of the chance, and invested in immense quantities of port, sherry, and Madeira, much of which is now beyond all price. Besides this, the Queen possesses the best collection in this country of East India sherry and Madeira and of Cabinet Rhine wines, while the value of the Imperial Tokay, which used to be much drunk in Prince Albert's time, is only exceeded by one or two of the wealthier Austrian and German princes.

The immense wine-cellars at Windsor are approached through an iron-barred gate, which jealously guards the cellar door on which is the number 571. A small office near at hand is used by the cellarman for keeping the accounts of the wine given out, and near this office hangs a bell which rings from within. The beer cellars, of which there are many, are all situated in or near to the sub-terranean passage that Prince Albert tunnelled under the Quadrangle.

Although her Majesty daily sees the rarest vintages served at her table, she has for many years contented herself with a small portion of Scotch whisky, which is distilled expressly for her near Balmoral, at the small distillery of John Begg, and which is carefully mixed by her personal attendant with either Apollinaris, soda, or Lithia water. In one thing, however, the Queen may be said to indulge quite freely, and that is tea. The tea consumed in the

Palaces costs four shillings a pound, and the Queen drinks the same as every one else. Whether Her Majesty helps to boil the kettle herself, or whether it is brought to her ready made, she always loves her tea. In the year 1887, when she honoured Sir Reginald Hanson, Bart., then Lord Mayor of London, with her presence at tea at the Mansion House, it was charming to watch her carefully remove her gloves, untie her bonnet strings, and fling them over her shoulders, preparatory to enjoying " the cup that cheers." Of coffee Her Majesty is not so very fond, though it is beautifully made by her servants.

When in Scotland the Queen is never averse to tasting the " Athole Brose," and on the completion of cairns at the Hallowe'en festivities and the simple country christenings and feasts Her Majesty so often attends, she will always, with true kindness, partake of the whisky that is handed round.

That the Queen, in spite of her own temperance—and I use the word in its truest and best sense—does not object to others enjoying themselves may be judged from the following incident, which occurred once on board the Royal yacht, *Victoria and Albert.* The Queen, who had been cruising in the Solent for some days, was sitting one fine morning on deck, plaiting straw for bonnets, then a most fashionable form of work. By and by she noticed a commotion among the sailors, who gathered in knots and seemed much perturbed. After a time, Lord Adolphus Fitz-Clarence, then in command of the yacht, was sent for by the men. The Queen, much puzzled, inquired if anything were wrong, and asked, jokingly, if a mutiny was afoot ? Lord Adolphus laughingly said that all would be well if the Queen would move her seat, and on being asked why she should, and what harm was she doing where she was, answered : " Well, ma'am, Your Majesty is unwittingly sitting in front of the door of the place where the grog is kept, and the men cannot get at their drink."

The Queen laughed, and consented to move on condition that some grog was brought to her. On tasting it she said : " I fear I can only repeat the remark that I made once before ; the grog would be much better if it were stronger."

The Queen, who always gets through a couple of hours' work between leaving her dinner guests and retiring to rest, invariably takes a " nightcap " before settling down for the night. But in her eating and drinking, as in all other conditions of life, the Queen has always set an example of self-control and restraint to all those about her.

THE INDIAN ROOM AT OSBORNE.

CHAPTER XVIII

THE QUEEN'S PETS

THE Queen's genuine love for almost all animals is
well known, but few people are aware of the deep
personal interest Her Majesty takes in her dumb creatures,
or can realise the thought and money that are expended on
their suitable lodging, proper food, and constant care. The
one exception to the Queen's large-hearted sympathy with
the animal kingdom is made with regard to cats. These
the Sovereign holds in the greatest abhorrence, and not
one of them is allowed to be where she is likely to see it.

On the other hand the Queen has a perfect adoration for
dogs, and a genuine love and appreciation for her many
horses.

Each individual animal belonging to the Queen is well
lodged and tended, for her Majesty argues that the possession of an animal renders the owner responsible for its
well-being. Hence it is that the Royal Stables at all the
Queen's houses are hygienically so perfect, and that the
Queen's Kennels in the Home Park at Windsor are valuable models of what healthy and cleanly houses for dogs
should be.

The Kennels are situated on a sunny slope and form a
picturesque attachment to the very pretty cottage in Gothic

style of the Keeper of the Queen's dogs, and of the plainly furnished room, which, according to custom, is kept sacredly apart for the exclusive·use of Her Majesty. The Kennels themselves are really a most beautifully built row of little houses, very white and clean in effect, and each with a wired inclosure or "run" before it. For cleaning and feeding purposes they can be entered from the back. Dogs with young families, and those of a breed who should be together, or who live with perfect unity one with the other, are placed together, but in no instance does one "kennel" or house contain more than three or four dogs.

Before the Kennels lies a splendid open piece of turf, divided by netting into large "runs." Here is a general mingling of dogs, and much gambolling, barking, and racing. When the Queen drives up to the Kennels, most of the animals are turned out on this lovely sward for her inspection. Besides this precarious exercise, all the dogs are taken in parties for a good walk in the Park every morning.

It is not to be expected that all this number of dogs are personal favourites of the Queen—although she knows and has named each individual animal—or that they are allowed the free run of her private apartments. Far from it. Many of the animals at the Royal Kennels are bred to give away, or are presents that have been pressed on Her Majesty. At the same time the Queen has seldom, if ever, concentrated her affection on one dog alone. In the Prince Consort's time (which was also the day of the graceful and faithful hound "Eos") the Queen's suite, when she moved anywhere, generally comprised at least half-a-dozen dogs. Skye terriers were then very popular with the Queen, and also turnspits. Of these last quaint creatures the Royal Kennels contain a great many fine specimens, which are descendants of some very well-bred animals brought by Prince Albert from Germany.

Of collies the Queen was always very fond, and she owns several fine dogs of this breed, though, being in most instances pure bred, they are not so attractive to English eyes as are those that are a cross between the collie and the Gordon setter. One of the pure white collies called " Lily " always travels with the Queen. The other, " Maggie," is not so pretty a creature. A fox-terrier called " Spot," and the perky little tan-coloured German Spitz-dog, " Marco," also are generally with the Queen. Marco's wife, " Lenda," is not so engaging as he is. His offspring are numerous and charming, and although the Queen has given many of them away, these Spitzes, in various shades of yellow and brown, are ubiquitous in the Royal Kennels.

The Queen possesses a pair of exquisite white Spitz-dogs. The male, called " Turri," was brought from Florence.

There is no doubt that Her Majesty's pet dog for many years was a collie named " Sharp." The Queen was devoted to this animal, who, when with his Royal Mistress, always behaved delightfully. He had all his meals with her, and but seldom left her side. Oddly enough, he was a most bad-tempered beast, and the Household and servants were, with the exception of John Brown, who kept him in some sort of order, terrified of him. One morning, as a servant was holding "Sharp" in readiness for the Queen to come out for her airing, the dog flew at him in a fit of temper. The man, half frightened, caught "Sharp" a heavy blow across the loins with a stick he carried. Her Majesty, seeing the dog walk lame, asked if he had been hurt, and the attendant, afraid to say that he had struck the animal, answered he had hurt his back in trying to jump up trees after squirrels. As "Sharp" always did this, the Queen was satisfied, but the dog limped at times to the day of his death.

Yet Her Majesty did acknowledge that her favourite had

a tendency to fight when out of doors, for she once mentioned that on an expedition " good Sharp " took in her company, he varied the monotony of the way by having numerous "collie-shangies," the vernacular in the Highlands for a row between collies.

" Noble " was another collie of whom the Queen was very fond. He always guarded her gloves, and was a most faithful friend. From time to time the Queen has shown some of her collies, but she is, as a rule, averse to exhibiting such sensitive creatures.

Very different is the case with the Queen's cattle. For many years the Windsor Farms, the Home, the Flemish, and the Shaw Farms, have produced the grandest prize-stock in the world, and the Queen is exceedingly proud of the fact. She takes the liveliest interest in the magnificent animals bred on her estates, and few of the splendid roan calves grow up to be fattened and killed without receiving many visits from the Queen. Not only in prize-bred animals does Her Majesty sweep the board, but also in fat stock. When the Royal Family used to spend all December and Christmastide at Windsor, the Queen and the Prince used, with the children and Household, to walk round the Farms frequently and inspect the fat stock, which is principally kept at the Shaw Farm. Nearer to the Castle is the very quaint, low-lying Flemish Farm where the dairy cows are kept and milked in a long double row of stalls, each labelled with its occupant's name. Here also for a time lived a wonderful buffalo, which had been sent to the Queen as a calf, and a very pretty little Albino pony which Her Majesty purchased from Hengler's Circus to please the little Princes of Battenberg.

All the Queen's cattle are washed over once a week with a mild and sweet disinfectant. The work is done by very experienced men from the time the creatures are young calves, and they grow to enjoy the process. The Queen's Farms are splendidly managed and more than pay for themselves, yet, though the Queen is so fond of her stock, the number kept is always rigorously cut down if winter food promises to be scarce or too expensive.

It is a pretty sight on all the Royal Farms to see the superannuated horses from the Queen's Stables quietly feeding in the sheltered paddocks or doing a little easy work. Every one of these good old servants the Queen knows by name, and notices as she takes her morning drives over her great property.

Quite close to Frogmore House, and just past that miracle of cleanliness and white marble, exquisite tile work and tinkling fountains that go to make up the Queen's Dairy, is the Royal Aviary, which, facing a sunny slope and hemmed in by a fine shrubbery, was built by the Prince Consort for such birds as the Queen might fancy to keep. It is a charming group of buildings, the centre being occupied by the Keeper's house, and containing a very little apartment where the Queen and her children used to go and drink tea. The Aviary faces a good-sized basin of water, into which the ducks and a pretty fountain splash all day long. Looking on to this pleasant scene are eighteen pens full of splendid poultry, all of the best breeds, as the blue labels affixed to each indicates. At the back are the perfectly arranged roosting and sitting houses.

Each breed of birds is kept carefully distinct, and it is amusing to watch a penful of silver spangled Hamburghs being driven home before either the Black Minorcas, Andalusians or any other kind are let out for an hour's run on the fresh turf.

The eggs served at the Queen's breakfast-table are exclusively those of white Dorkings.

All new and interesting breeds of poultry are at once patronised by Her Majesty, who nowadays frequently drives to the Aviary at feeding time to watch her grandchildren feed the birds. A splendid penful of gold-spangled Hamburgs belongs to little Prince Alexander of Battenberg, who is very proud of the handsome birds.

Of the number of birds raised every year at the Aviary, one hundred are always kept for stocking the pens the others being fattened for the Castle.

Of ducks the Queen has but few, and only about seventy Aylesbury ducks are reared a year for the Royal table.

Fancy birds include some seventy lovely pigeons, principally Jacobins, and foreign owls. Some pure white doves belong to Princess Beatrice, whose favourite birds are, however, canaries, of which a cageful accompanies her wherever she goes. Cinnamon turkeys are successfully bred at the Royal Aviary, and there are also some handsome golden pheasants.

Yet even more interesting than the live pets are the stuffed birds that in glass cases almost line the Queen's little sitting-room in the Keeper's cottage.

Here are Japanese, silver, and Amherst pheasants, an emu's head, some gorgeous Indian pigeons, and the magnificent peacock that once belonged to Lord Beaconsfield, and was sent to the Queen from Hughenden soon after his death. A great case contains some birds, capercailzie, black cock and grouse, shot by Prince Albert at " Taymouth, September 8th and 9th, 1842."

In Her Majesty's rooms at the Castle are some linnets of which she is very fond. Strange birds to possess, and scarcely to be regarded as pets, are two huge eagles, one caught in Windsor Forest and one in Scotland, that live in a large aviary at the Head Keeper's Lodge.

Whenever the Queen drinks tea with Mrs. Overstone at

the Lodge, she always inspects these Royal but unsociable birds.

Other queer animals owned by the Queen are some long-haired white Canadian pigs, and an inclosure full of wild boars in the forest. These last are most ferocious-looking animals. A few are killed at Christmas time, and their heads, after being suitably decorated by the *chefs*, are sent by the Queen to certain members of the Royal Family, while one figures on the sideboard at Osborne.

The Queen's kindness even to animals with which she has no personal association has always been great. In 1877, when she was driving up Glen Muick, near Balmoral, her people told her that a little fawn was lying at the bottom of a disused gravel-pit. The Queen had the exhausted animal rescued and brought to her, and insisted on having it in her carriage and bearing it in her own arms back to the Castle. The animal was named "Victoria," and lived for ten years on the Balmoral estate.

This same kindness she inculcated in all her children, and Princess Alice, on one of her birthdays, found her greatest pleasure in a pet lamb, all pink ribbons and bells. She afterwards wept bitterly because the lamb would not love her so much as she loved it.

Nearly all the Queen's pet animals have been perpetuated, and her rooms everywhere contain pictures, and statuettes in marble, gold, or silver of her favourite horses and dogs. "Sharp" was modelled several times and once taken in company with the Queen on her Throne. Memories of the faithful "Eos" are everywhere. "Boy" and "Boz," in bronze are embowered among flowers near the Dairy. "Noble," I have already said, faces "Eos" below the North Terrace. One of the grandest gold centre-pieces the Queen has, is a group of five of her pet dogs ; another is made up of portrait models of four favourite steeds. On all the Queen's estates are touching tablets to the memory of some faithful dumb friend. The Queen has loved them all, and nothing can hurt her more than cruelty to animals or an unjust depreciation of their many virtues.

CHAPTER XIX

THE QUEEN'S RELIGION AND HER SUNDAY OBSERVANCE

ON the memorable morning of June 20, 1837, when the Archbishop of Canterbury (Dr. Howley), and the Lord Chamberlain, the Marquis of Conyngham, toil-worn and dust-stained with their night ride from Windsor, beat at the doors of Kensington Palace—as the present writer has often heard the late Marquis describe—at five o'clock, and announced to the awakened girl of eighteen that she was the Queen of England, she kissed the extended hands of the kneeling messengers and fell on her knees between them, saying : " I ask your prayers on my behalf."

This would have been an extraordinary sentiment in any ordinary little lady, but it came naturally from one who we hear from her preceptor, Bishop Davis of Peterborough, had had the Bible read to her every day, and the anecdote is typical of the Queen's entire life, for those who know her well would be only too ready to admit that she is a deeply religious woman, who in all temptations and trials, tribulations and triumphs, has put her faith in God's grace and who marks all acts of her private and public life by a prayerful appeal, and has brought up her children in the love and fear of God.

Nor is Her Majesty by any means intolerant, as too

many are—nor could any one with truth accuse her of fanaticism. Neither has the Queen ever permitted religion and the strict observance of religious forms to turn her sympathies from the natural inclinations of humanity and the duties of her state in life. Indeed, humanity may be said to be her strongest characteristic, for there is none of her subjects who has a more keen appreciation of fun and the affairs of the world generally than Her Majesty.

It is not, however, the more worldly side of Her Majesty's life with which I am at present concerned. Whatever may follow or has been said depicting the other six days of the Queen's working week, my mission is now with the first day of the week and its observance.

Sunday is with Her Majesty, in the best sense of the phrase, a day of rest. On Sunday she never transacts business of any kind nor allows her servants, whether they be ministers or maids, to execute other than the most necessary duties. Did space permit or necessity demand, I could illustrate this characteristic by quite a number of anecdotes.

I have used the expression "in the best sense of the phrase," and it may be as well to explain exactly what I mean by it. The Queen does not regard the due observance of Sunday by what she well calls "a moping over good books," but by what she terms in a finer and better sense, "being and doing good."

The Queen's own form of worship is Church of England, with a strong leaning towards Presbyterianism, which latter inclination may be accounted for partly by Scotch influence, partly by the Prince Consort's Lutheran training, and partly by her own love of simplicity in all things that surround and appertain to herself, whether it be manners, speech, or even the patterns of her curtains.

The Queen has never attended any High Church public

service, nor permitted the private services she attends to be conducted with the aid of vestments, candles, processions, or other ornamental accessories. Indeed, her greatest delight was to attend the poor little church at Crathie and to communicate after the Presbyterian manner in her turn with the rest of the simple Highland congregation. And it was only her horror at finding that her presence turned the service into a show and an attraction to staring tourists that made her abandon Whippingham Church and set up a private Prayer-room at Osborne House.

The Queen's Private Chapel at Windsor Castle is in no way accessible to other than especially privileged visitors, and is therefore unknown to the general public who are permitted to inspect the State Apartments during Her Majesty's absence.

It was formerly the music-room of the Queen's private band, but was converted to its present use by the Prince Consort, and consecrated by the Dean of Westminster, the Rev. Samuel Wilberforce, afterwards Bishop of Oxford, on December 19, 1843. This is recorded on a scroll held by the carved wooden statue of an angel, immediately outside the Queen's private pew, in the following words : " This Chapel was altered and decorated under the direction of H.R.H. the Prince Consort in the fifth year of the reign of Queen Victoria."

It will be more convenient, for the purposes of description, for the reader to enter in spirit by the Visitors' Entrance in the Quadrangle, as it is from the small vestibule at the head of the Visitors' Stairs that the Queen's own entrance to her private pew, up a small winding white and gold staircase, springs. Despite many announcements in the papers of late, this ascension has in no way been levelled, nor would such an alteration, perhaps, be possible.

The Queen's pew and the pew of Her Majesty's visitors,

which are joined by a narrow arched doorway, are on a level with the organ, about twelve feet from the floor. The Queen's pew is shut off from the private staircase and the private retiring gallery by a screen of frosted glass and white painted wood of Gothic style. For want of a better simile, these pews may be likened to private boxes in a theatre, which in size and shape they resemble. Their design is pure Gothic, the arches being relieved by gold. They are simply furnished with a few chairs and hassocks, the upholstery being red velvet stamped with "V.R." which matches the red carpet. In the centre of each hangs from the ceiling a large ormolu lamp, the frosted glass panes of which are relieved by a large "V.R."

The back and side walls are emblazoned with small heraldic shields, Her Majesty's pew holding ten and the Visitors' pew eight. Like all other apartments in the Castle the Queen's pew boasts a thermometer.

Descending the Queen's private staircase, we come to a small door on the left, and three steps lead us up to a narrow slip of an apartment which contains, perhaps, the most unique and priceless collection by Holbein, Janet, and other Dutch masters, set round the walls in white panels. Here also, on a small bracket, is a lovely little brass clock, which was given by Henry VIII. to Anne Boleyn on the morning of her marriage.

Passing through this dim, if not very religious, little art gallery, we come to the oak doors of the Chapel, which, being opened, admit us to the ground floor and the pews under the organ occupied by the ladies and gentlemen of the Household.

The Chapel itself is Gothic in style, and principally lit from the lantern roof of glass set in stone mullions, the lines of which are lightly touched with gold. From the floor upwards for twelve feet a handsome oak and gilt wainscot has a somewhat sombre warm effect, which helps to mitigate the severe plainness of the upper portion of the white walls.

The East window is divided into six panels of stained glass, the subjects being the Saviour surrounded by the Evangelists and St. Peter, the whole framed by four smaller panels of angels.

The reredos is handsomely designed in a charming blending of coloured marbles. The altar, flanked on either side by carved oak chairs marked with the entwined initials "I.H.S." and "X.P.," is characteristically simple, as are also the rails.

The most striking feature in the immediate vicinity is the pulpit, which is on the right, and is entered directly by a door leading from the vestry, and is surmounted by a very graceful and beautiful oak canopy, carved in Gothic style. The reading-desk on the other side is much plainer.

A strong decorative note is struck by the organ, a magnificent instrument elaborately ornamented in white and gold, which stands in a fine carved and gilt oak gallery.

This organ, which has a double action, is used when concerts are given in St. George's Hall.

The principal way of artificially lighting the Chapel is afforded by a magnificent brass chandelier of elaborate and most graceful Gothic form. It is suspended from the lantern roof by thick brass chains, and supports twelve oil lamps, Her Majesty disliking gas and not taking kindly to the electric light. The arrangement of the pews, which are of oak (each being furnished with a red-plush cushion stamped "V.R." and four red carpet covered hassocks) is very irregular.

Besides those under the organ on the left or north side which have been already designated, those on the right and left of the centre aisle are occupied by the footmen, house-maids, etc. Those round the south or right-hand wall are reserved for the pages and visitors' servants, and that in the north-west corner for the Housekeeper and upper servants.

Two small pews to the right and left of the door facing the altar are respectively reserved for the use of the Queen's Private Secretary and Lady Biddulph, the latter being dis-tinguished by the beautifully modelled terra cotta group by Dalou of a winged angel surrounded by five children, representing the Queen's grandsons who died in infancy.

To left and right of the reading desk and pulpit are two bronze bas-reliefs, portraits of Dean Wellesley and Dean Stanley. By the side of the memorial to Dean Wellesley is a tablet which has the following inscription :

" In affectionate remembrance of Major General Sir Howard Elphinstone, K.C.B., C.M.G., V.C., born 12th December, 1829, lost at sea 8th March, 1890. This memorial has been placed here by the Queen as a grateful recognition of his services to Her Majesty and to her son, the Duke of Connaught. ' In the midst of life we are in death.' "

There are also, on the south and west walls, memorial tablets to General Grey, the Queen's favourite Private Secretary, and Sir Thomas Biddulph.

So much for the Queen's Chapel at Windsor.

The Prayer-room at Osborne is far simpler in design and arrangement, and, except for the very plain pulpit and altar, its surrounding furniture and the small organ is quite devoid of ecclesiastical suggestion, as neither reading-desk nor lectern finds a place there. The Prayer-room is reached from the Queen's Private Apartments by a long corridor on the first floor, and an open *loggia* which gives on a staircase. A small ante-room at the foot of the stair-case is adorned with sacred pictures painted on china plaques. The room itself—for it is nothing more—is lighted by lofty windows overlooking the beautiful Upper and Lower Terraces. The carpet and hangings are crimson, and the woodwork of highly polished walnut. The altar is very small, and is mainly noticeable for the three pictures that hang above it: "A Man of Sorrows," "Vigilate et Orate," and "The Good Shepherd," all by Sir Noel Paton. Between the windows are a "Virgin and Child," and "The Redeemer Enthroned," by Sarabino, and some charming studies of angels' heads. No pews cumber the floor of the Prayer-room. The front row of chairs, which are armed and cushioned, are used by the Royal party, the Queen sitting the third from the right, and having a small table before her. The Household and servants sit on chairs in rows behind Her Majesty

Her Majesty attends the short twelve to one o'clock service regularly, and prefers that those members of the Household whose "wait" it is should also be in attendance.

The Service consists of what is known as the Morning Service, namely, the litany, a hymn, the ante-communion, a hymn, and a short sermon. The Queen prefers discourses of about twenty minutes, and has no sympathy with the modern style of introducing æsthetics, economics, or politics into the pulpit.

She much prefers a plain exposition of practical truths arising out of some subject of the day, and is known to favour unwritten sermons.

The same form of arrangement prevails in the Prayer-room at Balmoral, which the Queen has used now for some years, only going occasionally to the quaint old Crathie Church, to supplant which a larger edifice is in course of construction.

The Queen, though still clinging to many of the simpler forms of worship enjoined by the Presbyterian Church, has relaxed of late years to some extent her almost Puritanical observance of the Sabbath. That she should have done this is only another example of her extraordinarily broad and liberal mind. The Queen, for all her particularity, has never been a bigot. As long ago as July, 1834, Dr. Howley, the Archbishop of Canterbury, who then confirmed the Princess Victoria in the Chapel Royal, St. James's, said "that she was too intrinsically religious by nature to ever be affected by the mere outward forms of worship."

There is one point, however, on which Her Majesty has been, and always will be, inflexible. No matter of what opinion or what rank in the Church the preacher of the day may be, he must wear a black gown when delivering his sermon before the Queen.

The Queen has always shown a strong partiality for the clergy. She loves to talk of the many great churchmen who assisted in the moulding of her character and in her education ; and her dinner-party on Sunday, to which the preacher of the day is invariably commanded, is always marked by much reminiscence.

It would be impossible to enumerate all Her Majesty's favourite hymns, but among those which are especially asked for are Toplady's "Rock of Ages," "To Thee, O Lord," "I shall not in the grave remain," "Thy Will be done," "Happy Soul, thy days are ended," which has been so beautifully set by H.R.H. Prince Consort, and Mendelssohn's "Hear my Prayer," which was an especial favourite of the late Duke of Albany.

The simple little service in the Queen's Private Chapel is a very solemn and impressive experience, never to be forgotten by those who have had the privilege of attending it, while to those who can recall the more imposing appearance of the Queen when, with her husband and children, and surrounded by her Court, she worshipped at the Chapel

Royal, or at the Private Chapel at Buckingham Palace, the quiet modesty of her present surroundings is infinitely touching. In face of such staunch Protestantism as the Queen professes, it is almost grotesque to go back to the early years of her reign, when men, both in England and Ireland, were base enough to accuse Her Majesty of the intention of re-establishing the Papacy as the National religion.

That the Queen had no such intentions nor ideas she has proved throughout her entire life, though at the same time she has been tolerant of all faiths, and during her tour in Ireland in 1849 was much struck and pleased with the broad-mindedness shown by those who had the direction of the model schools in Dublin. The Roman Catholic Archbishop himself conducted Her Majesty over the schools, where she found that no one creed was paramount, and where, as she herself remarked : " The Gospel truths, Love and Charity, were the only religion enforced." The Queen has since frequently said, that she would it had been the same in all schools.

In the Sacrament of Baptism the Queen takes a truly Christian interest, and when she is at Balmoral no little soul is sealed to Christ without her substantial approbation and frequently her personal attendance.

One very terrible trial came to the Queen through her strong and fervent religion. Some time after her marriage to the Grand Duke of Hesse, Princess Alice, the Queen's dearest daughter, showed strong signs of wavering from the faith in which she had been so carefully brought up. The Princess was naturally deeply religious, but her own serious and thoughtful nature, coupled with the circumstances of her life, led her first to question and then to falter. For some months a most interesting correspondence passed between the Princess and the Queen, the letters of the latter being most touching in their solicitude for her daughter's spiritual welfare. That the Princess' beautiful and trusting nature returned to the faith in which she was reared and that she died in it, a devout Christian, proved a consolation to the Queen, who has ever placed her religion and the welfare of her soul above the mere earthly considerations of crowns and kingdoms.

CHAPTER XX

MUCH of the Queen's heavy daily work is self-imposed, and, from the point of view of governing her great Empire, absolutely unnecessary. When Her Majesty has, in her pretty open tent at Osborne, or beneath the shadow of the two splendid evergreen oaks at Frogmore, finished considering State papers, signing the despatches, and dictating letters on every conceivable subject, she turns to the vast pile of purely family and private correspondence which awaits her perusal every twenty-four hours. Apart from State business, it has been proved that the Queen is the greatest correspondent of the day, not only as regards the letters she receives and reads, but those she indites with her own hand in reply.

A point on which the Queen is extremely punctilious is the insistence that, unless debarred by illness, all her children and grandchildren shall write to her once in every day. These letters are not merely scrappy effusions made up of commonplaces and trivialities, but partake more of the nature of diaries, noting not only every event in the writer's life, but the thoughts and sensations entailed thereby.

Her Majesty is herself a most introspective letter-writer, and only cares for letters of a like quality.

The Queen does not answer *all* her family correspondence every day, for to do so would be a task beyond even her powers, but any letters that deal with sorrow or joy, doubts and fears, or hopes and anticipations, always meet with a speedy and intensely sympathetic reply from this true " head " of her family. The Queen's letters written to her descendants, under various and important trying circumstances, are most beautiful compositions, and imbued with a love and tenderness that is almost not of this world. In these days letter writing is a lost art to almost every one save Her Majesty, who has preserved unimpaired her extraordinary aptitude in this particular.

The Queen's letters to the nation, which in moments of national rejoicing or grief she has from time to time indited in a spirit of thanksgiving or sympathy, are in themselves monuments of consideration, self-restraint, and good taste, in fact, altogether admirable. But I venture to say that were the Queen's letters to her family and friends made public, they would astound the whole literary world, and at once take rank among the standard works of all time.

Among the many beautiful letters written by the Queen must not be forgotten the long and touching effusion she penned to the Prince of Wales on his eighteenth birthday, announcing to him his emancipation from parental control. It was full of affectionate warnings and prayers for his future, and was pronounced by those few who saw it as being the most beautiful letter ever written. The Prince himself was so deeply moved by it that he burst into a flood of tears on showing it to the Rev. Gerald Wellesley. Her letters to her daughter, Princess Alice, after her marriage, and her daily communications to the Dowager Empress of Germany during the long and terrible illness of the Emperor Frederick, are incomparable in their tenderness and sympathy.

The letters written by the Queen to her Ministers—or

to reduce the matter to facts, by a woman to some of the greatest men of the century—were always remarkable for their clearness of expression, grasp of situation and detail and for strong decision. Her Majesty never used two words where one would serve, she never alternated or prevaricated, her choice of expression was always to the point, and she has never been known to commit that too common fault of her sex—interlarding business matters with extraneous and unnecessary remarks.

Lord John Russell—who from time to time had political differences with the Queen—received from her on more than one occasion letters of the firmest and most authoritative character, indicating clearly that Her Majesty could express her displeasure on paper as forcibly as she could her other sensations.

The Queen's letters of condolence in times of great grief have been penned by her own hand to many of her subjects, and have by their sweetness and sympathy brought balm to many a wounded heart. When her music mistress, Mrs. Anderson, who had also taught all the elder of the Queen's children to play the piano, lost her husband, who for years had been the master of Her Majesty's private band, her greatest consolation grew out of the touching letter written by her Royal pupil and friend.

In lighter vein were the very pretty letters written to members of her Household concerning happy events. The lines penned to the Hon. Georgiana Liddell, a Maid of Honour, on her marriage, are delightful in their cordiality and womanly kindness.

When the Queen first came to the throne a great deal of her private correspondence was conducted by her former governess, Baroness Lehzen, but the Prince Consort, who was an indefatigable letter writer, encouraged the Queen to use her own hand for her more intimate letters.

Once only—outside periods of illness—did the Queen ever lose touch with all business and private affairs. That was at the time of the Prince Consort's death, when for some weeks every communication passed through the hands of Princess Alice. The tribute paid by the *Times* to this young Princess, who was herself overwhelmed with grief at her father's death, was in itself a monument to her bravery and goodness.

Almost the first letter penned by the Queen after her great grief, was that to the nation, which few can even now read dry-eyed, so touching and sad is it.

During the last few years the Queen confided a great deal of her more confidential correspondence to the late Sir Henry Ponsonby, from whom she had few, if any, secrets. Sir Henry Ponsonby had a splendid house within the Castle walls in the Norman Tower, but he also had two apartments, a sitting-room and bedroom, leading off from the Marble Hall and overlooking the North Terrace. They are plainly furnished, comfortable rooms, which are used by the Queen's Private Secretary at busy times.

They are close to the office, where a staff of clerks is always at work, and quite near the little telegraph office, through which pass in cipher the secrets of all nations.

The Royal Mail Bag is a very bulky affair, and is first gone through by the Private Secretary. Letters from lunatics and beggars and people filled with impertinent curiosity are daily items in the correspondence, but all are sorted and answered courteously. A certain proportion of begging letters are set before the Queen, but to attain this preference they must be clearly written on thick-glazed paper and be neither folded or rolled.

Family letters are conveyed unopened to Her Majesty. Such letters as do not come in the province of the Private Secretary to answer, or which the Queen does not care to write, are confided to the most trusted of the Maids of Honour, or, if very confidential, to a favourite Lady-in-Waiting. Naturally, absolute silence respecting the contents of such letters is expected and preserved.

Protests to foreign nations are sometimes laid before the Queen by Ministers, and when they advise, are written by her own hand.

The Queen's handwriting is pointed, sloping, and clear. It was always larger and more virile in character than the fashionable " Italian " hand of her youthful days, and was strangely like the writing of the Prince Consort. Her first baby signature in printed letters is preserved in the British Museum.

All letters received by the Queen are kept and filed. Her private and family correspondence is, however, always under lock and key in certain cabinets. The letters of the day are brought to her in various despatch boxes, covered with morocco, bearing the Royal cipher on the lid.

The letter-paper used by Her Majesty herself is commendably plain. It is of the thickest and richest cream-laid, narrowly edged with black, and bearing at the top the Queen's cipher, surmounted by a crown and the name of her residence from which the letter is written, both being stamped in black. The Royal Arms and the name of the palace decorate all other paper and envelopes used in the household.

It is not generally known that all the Queen's letters from her own hand are written in English.

As a speller Her Majesty is exceedingly accurate, and, where names are concerned, very precise. A little anecdote illustrates this.

For many years the Queen was much put out by the perpetual variation in the Foreign Office and other despatches of the spelling of the titles of the Sovereigns

of Russia.   She always punctiliously used the words,
Tsar and Tsarina, and frequently remonstrated with those
who spelt the words indifferently as Czar and Czarina.   At
length the late Sir Henry Ponsonby, who was the Queen's
private secretary, wrote himself to the Foreign Office and
said that if the clerks there could not spell the word
Tsarevitch properly they had better send to Newmarket
to inquire how it should be written.

It was at one time rather the fashion to decry the Queen's
powers as an authoress—or rather as an expressive writer.
Those who did so were neither judges of style nor of method.
The writings of the Queen's which the public have been
permitted to see have essentially the elements of great work,
perfect simplicity of expression, and admirable self-restraint.
The Queen never gushes or over-writes, and of what other
feminine writer can such words be truly said?   She has a
great pictorial power, and her descriptions of scenery are
first-rate.   Also Her Majesty has a fine sense of humour
and an infinite appreciation of sorrow, and these are two
vital elements in good writing.

Of her pathos in writing it is impossible to speak too
highly.   The entire description of the last hours and
death of her mother, the Duchess of Kent, as written
by the Queen's own hand, is one of the most graphic
and moving passages ever penned in the English language.

The many inscriptions to the memory of dear friends
and faithful servants are what such things should ever
be, sincere and grateful.

If the Queen had been destined by Fate to write in lieu
of ruling, she must have left a great mark on the literature
of the century.

CHAPTER XXI

THE COURT LIFE OF A MAID OF HONOUR

IN the eyes of the public the post and duties of the Queen's Maids of Honour are both unimportant and insignificant. By turning to the list of the Queen's Household, and comparing the salaries of its many members, which are set forth fully in any good work of general information, the curious in such matters discover that the emolument of a Maid of Honour is comparatively small, and on the usual line of a world that values every one according to his wealth or income, they infer that the duties are correspondingly trifling.

A greater mistake could not well be made. Now that Her Majesty has so greatly curtailed her state, and limits so strictly the number of those about her, the Maids of Honour are not only extremely busy members of Court, but also have to perform duties which in happier times were executed by a greater number of people. Yet at no period of the Queen's reign were her Maids of Honour merely ornamental appendages to her state. From the very first moment that the young Queen's ministers and advisers went into debate over the subject of Her Majesty's Household, their Royal Mistress put her foot down and insisted that all the young ladies about her person should conform to certain requirements. It is a noteworthy fact that for the past sixty years no deviation has been made from the rules laid down which, in the first month of the Queen's reign, regulated the choice, position, and duties of the Maid of Honour.

Few people realise that about these duties there is a great sense of mystery. Maids of Honour are brought into the most intimate contact with the Sovereign, and it is, therefore, a *sine quâ non* that they should preserve the utmost reticence about their life at Court. Nobody outside the charmed circle can have any just idea of the thousand and one small businesses and pleasures of the Queen's life, and it is with a view of lifting the veil somewhat that I consider an epitome of a Maid of Honour's "wait" may prove of considerable interest.

Before, however, treating on what is, it may be well by way of contrast, to touch on what was.

There is no doubt that for many centuries the Court life of England was sullied by the conduct of the Court ladies, among whom the "Maids" were, as a rule, the most beautiful and the most daring. The Court was merely a market-place where a girl of noble birth might carry her charms, and sell them to the highest bidder. In Elizabeth's time some restraint was put upon the hitherto unbridled license of the Maids of Honour, but in James I.'s reign this was again relaxed. Henrietta Maria, the Queen of Charles I., made a very strong effort to cleanse that Augean Stables— the English Court—and the following strict rules were drawn up in 1625, and enforced by her orders :

"The Queen's Maids of Honour are to come into the Presence Chamber before eleven of the clock, and to go to prayers, and after prayers to attend till the Queen be set at dinner. Again, at two o'clock to return into the said chamber, and there to remain until supper time. And when they shall be retired into their chamber they admit no man to come there, and that they go not at any time out of the Court without leave asked of the Lord Chamberlain, or Her Majesty, and that the Mother of the Maids see all these orders concerning the Maids duly observed, as she will answer to the contrary."

Of the conduct of the Maids of Honour to Charles II.'s unfortunate and neglected Queen it is not necessary to speak, so much of it being history, but it is certain that the abuses and scandals of Court life reached their climax in that and the following reigns.

The Queens of the early Georges were content to have a number of fat, good-natured young women about their persons, and after George IV.'s separation from his Queen the feminine influence at his Court was anything but desirable. Queen Adelaide, the Consort of William IV., was too short a time in power to really probe the rottenness of her surroundings to the bottom, and it was left to a young and tender-hearted girl of eighteen to at once make a clean sweep of the past abuses, and inaugurate and supervise a method of work and sympathy and loving kindness which has made the Court of Queen Victoria the crowning jewel of purity in all her great reign.

And yet, strangely enough, the initial details of choosing a young lady for the onerous post of Maid of Honour are almost identical with those which prevailed when the English Court was a by-word among all nations.

A girl to be eligible for this unique and confidential position must primarily be of good birth, though by no means, as some people imagine, the daughter of a peer. Her father or mother have probably already been in the Queen's service, sometimes an aunt or elder sister have themselves served as Maids of Honour. At any rate, whatever her own position, her choice as a Maid at once gives her the courtesy title of " Honourable," which she is allowed

to retain all her life, and even should she marry—a con-
tingency that oddly enough does not very often come in the
way of the Queen's Maids.

Next to the question of suitable birth comes that of
accomplishments. Her Majesty requires both variety and
perfection. A Maid of Honour must be able to speak, read,
and write French and German without a fault, she must also
understand a little Latin, while as regards her own language,
her grammar and pronunciation must be above reproach.
She must write quickly in a clear, "lady-like" hand, for the
Queen has a rooted dislike to any affectations of masculinity.
A very clear voice, good expression and enunciation are also
necessary, for nowadays most of the Queen's reading is done
for her, and a Maid must be ready to read a written report
on business matters, the newspapers, books, poetry, and
plays, with equal sense and readiness.

A knowledge of music is also quite necessary, and a Maid
to be popular with the Queen must be able both to sing and
play any style of music at sight, for Her Majesty frequently
has a pile of new songs or a whole opera played to her
during an evening.   At one time she herself frequently
played and sang with her Maids, and she was and is a
most critical though just supervisor of all musical efforts.
Until a few years back a Maid of Honour was always obliged
to be an accomplished and plucky horsewoman, for the
Queen was passionately fond of riding, and always required
the Maid of the moment to go with her.   One young lady
who was ignorant of this went to her first "wait" at Court
without a riding-habit, and on being commanded to ride
with the Queen was terribly distressed at the omission in
her wardrobe.   Her Majesty, however, was not at all put
out, and at once lent her one of her own habits, hat, collar,
and cuffs. The young Maid, in a *naïve* letter to her mother,
said that considering the difference between Her Royal

Mistress' figure and her own, the habit fitted wonderfully, after she had "pinned it over in front." It is characteristic of Her Majesty's simplicity of character and child-like good nature that she should have gone riding for two hours and a quarter in company with a Maid of Honour whose habit bodice was pinned up in front.

For the rest a Maid of Honour must have a knowledge of games, a little sketching, and of needlework, for the Queen cannot bear to see idle hands about her. She is expected to be cheerful in manner and looks, willing and quick, and absolutely punctual. It is also expected that her lips shall be invariably sealed concerning the private life of her Royal Mistress, and regarding such business as may be intrusted to her to perform. Light talk, frivolous behaviour, and even a suspicion of scandal-mongering are entirely tabooed at Court, and, if persisted in, would first incur the gravest reproof, and afterwards a dispensation with the services.

But Her Majesty does not wish her Maids to be always at work. She encourages them in acting, the art of imitation (the Queen is very fond of a good bit of mimicry), and in dancing. She used to be very fond of herself teaching her Maids different kinds of steps and figures, and nowadays will always send for anything a new Maid of Honour may desire to see, or for any particular article that Her Majesty may wish to show her.

There are eight Maids of Honour, and their individual salaries are £300 a year. They "wait," two together, for a period of a month three times a year. The tie, therefore, for a young lady of no occupation is not very considerable. Maids of Honour are chosen by the Queen herself from among those who are suitable for the post. It should be mentioned that all the Queen's Maids have been known to her from their childhood upwards, and she is thus enabled, by personal observation, which with Her Majesty is exceedingly sharp and quick, to gather if they will prove useful and pleasant companions to her. The procedure of their appointment is very simple. A letter is sent to the parents of the young lady, requesting as a personal favour to the Queen she may be permitted to attend at Court. It is needless to remark that a complaisant answer is invariably sent in reply. After that the newly - chosen Maid awaits from the Lord Chamberlain the command for her first " wait."

The Mother of the Maids being now abolished, it is the Lady-in-Waiting who receives the new Maid and gives her hints as to her duties. The apartments of the Maids of Honour (two bedrooms and a sitting-room, which they both share) are close to the Lady-in-Waiting's rooms, and when off duty they generally sit together. The first thing brought to the Maid of Honour is her badge, which is a miniature picture of the Queen set in brilliants and suspended to a ribbon. Just before the dinner-hour the Maid of Honour in waiting has to stand in the corridor outside the Queen's private apartments. She carries a bouquet, which on entering the dining-room she lays at the right hand of the Queen's plate. The Maid of Honour sits at dinner next to the gentleman on the Queen's right.

It is highly necessary, therefore, that she should be a conversationalist, and always cognisant of the latest question of the hour. When Royal guests, however, are present, the Maid of Honour is placed farther away from Her Majesty.

The Maid of Honour stands near the person of the Sovereign until she retires to her private apartments, when the Maid is free to go to her own rooms, whence she is often sent for to play, sing, read, or take a hand at cards.

The Queen always calls her Maids by their Christian names, they addressing her as " Ma'am." She keeps quite *au fait* with their family affairs, and takes a warm interest in all that concerns them. It being sometimes rumoured that Maids of Honour are worked to death, have long hours of standing, and the dullest of lives, it is well to say that this is not so. The Queen is most considerate about her people, even to the extent of once refusing to have her Maid of Honour with her on an occasion when she had reason to believe her life would be attempted.

During the Prince Consort's lifetime, however, Her Majesty was far more strict—though equally kind—with her Maids than she has been since his death. Without her leave they were never permitted to sit in the Prince's presence, or address any remark to him. There was also at one time much comment on the fact that the Maids of Honour were always obliged to open the door for Prince Albert.

The Queen always takes a great interest in the clothes of her Maids, and never forgets a gown that has pleased her. As regards their dress, the ladies about the Court are obliged to dress well but very plainly, the Queen having a great objection to smart frocks, fly-away hats, and, above all, untidily-dressed hair. She often gives her Maids of Honour presents of jewellery, and frequently orders flowers for their personal adornment to be taken to their rooms.

Life at the Royal palaces is extremely regular. A Maid of Honour once wrote, *à propos* of Court life: " It always strikes me as so odd when I come back into waiting. Everything else changes, but the life here never does, and is always exactly the same from day to day and year to year." It is a great excitement, therefore, when on grand occasions the castle is very full, and the Maids of Honour have to vacate their own apartments and move into less commodious quarters for a few days. One rule only survives from those made in the seventeenth century. No male visitors, whether a member of the household or a near relation of a Maid of Honour, is ever allowed in the Maid's apartments. They may receive ladies in their own rooms, but gentlemen are seen by them in a comfortable room set apart for the purpose.

That a more than common bond grows between the Queen and her Maids is shown by the fact that many of them, after they have left their posts, return again and again to Court as visitors to, and dear friends of, the Queen.

CHAPTER XXII

THE QUEEN'S GOLD AND SILVER PLATE

APART from the interest which necessarily attaches
to articles which are in daily and intimate use by
our beloved Sovereign, the plate at Windsor Castle is
acknowledged the finest collection in the world, and is
more than worthy of consideration. The two so-called
Pantries—which in reality are strong-rooms of the most
approved and well-arranged kind—are separated from one
another by the plate-cleaning rooms, which are furnished
with all kinds of known appliances for the adequate polishing
and burnishing of every kind of rare and delicate goldsmith's
work. All the Royal plate is carried to these rooms in
rotation and cleaned whether in use or not, and the system
employed for giving it out and receiving it back forms ample
and responsible work for the Yeomen of the Pantries and
their assistants, many of whom are veritable giants among
men, as the weights that have to be moved are very often
enormous.

The Silver Pantry is nearest to the two plate-cleaning
rooms. A very thick iron door, which bears upon its
surface the inevitable little brass tablet engraved with a
number surmounted by a small crown, gives direct entrance
to the Pantry, which is a medium-sized room, lined from

floor to ceiling with deep cupboards of mahogany and glass. A window crossed with thick bars, and guarded at night by a heavy shutter, faces the door. A high narrow table runs down the centre of the room, and above it swing three oil lamps, for no gas is used in these particular rooms. Of other furniture or fittings the room is innocent, and with good reason. Every available inch of space behind the clear glass doors is crowded with articles of silver, while the centre table itself is piled high with parts of a silver dinner service that was in use the previous evening.

There are two full silver dinner services, one called the "Lion," the other the "Crown" service, by reason of the design of the handles of the covers. Otherwise they are practically alike, and are frequently used together.

The sixty-seven dozens of plates and the many scores of dishes all have the beautiful gadroon edge, while all the entrée dishes are square and stand on four feet. The heating arrangement beneath the entrée dishes is unique, consisting as it does of a tiny lamp of solid silver, in which a taper of pure wax is fixed. Among several dozens of silver sauce-boats are some with three slender feet that are very light in design. When the silver dinner service is used, the "table-deckers" ornament the table with pierced silver flower vases of many shapes.

These are arranged on plaques of plate glass set in a heavy, pierced, silver rim. The centre of the table may either bear the Jubilee "humble offering" of Lord and Lady Rothschild, which is a gigantic silver bowl of a shallow shape and a glorified "melon" design; the more beautiful oxidised silver vase of Etruscan form and covered with a whirling crowd of Bacchantes that was the Jubilee Cup at the Agricultural Show; or perhaps the lovely George III. bowl presented to the Queen by the Charterhouse boys in the Jubilee year.

The glass case immediately on your left hand as you enter is filled with innumerable silver tea services. Many of them are alike in pattern, and most of the tea-pots have little silver strainers dangling from their spouts. A remarkable object in this same cupboard is a beautifully-modelled pair of birds—a cock and a hen—on a stand. Their backs are hollowed out to hold an egg. This is called the "chicken egg-cup," and it always stands on the Queen's breakfast table. So "intimate" to the Queen is it, that it figures prominently in the pretty picture of " Marco," her Majesty's favourite Spitz dog, which was hung in the Academy 1893. With this egg-cup is used the dainty little salt-cellar of a square shape in Russian silver, presented by Lady Alice Stanley to the Queen in 1877.

The case opposite this contains some fine silver cruets of Charles II., Anne, and George III. periods, a pair of little brandy-heaters that are always sent to Osborne at Christmas-time, and a beautiful pair of dishes for roasted chestnuts. They are of frosted silver, in the shape of a folded napkin, powdered with roses, thistles, and shamrocks. These dishes were presented to the Queen by Napoleon III. and the Empress Eugénie, and go to the Queen's table every night that chestnuts are in season.

Against the red baize background of the large cupboard that fills the right side of the room hang eight sconces in frosted silver. They bear the Garter insignia in polished silver and hold two candles a-piece. On a level with the ground is an extraordinary array of silver table candlesticks. There are one hundred and eighty pairs, and these are frequently all in use. Of bedroom candlesticks there are many shelves full. Each has a pair of snuffers pertaining to it, but these are never used, with the exception of two pairs that are sent to the Queen's apartments when she is at Windsor A quaint little flat candlestick with a peculiarly long, straight handle, is used by the Princess Beatrice when at Windsor.

A very handsome oak case standing at the end of the table and facing the window contains the large set of silver dessert dishes given by the Royal servants to the Queen at her Jubilee.

A very handsome, although plain, kettle on a high stand, all in solid silver, was used by the Prince Consort as a "dressing-kettle," but since his death has never left its case except to be cleaned.

Thirty triple-light candelabra have been added to the Silver Pantry during the present reign, and the enormous "shell pattern" service of knives, forks and spoons has also been largely augmented. Of reading candles and lamps, trays, small bowls, vases, salt-cellars, and inkstands there are an infinity. Among the last-named, a small, flat, round stand, pierced with places for quill pens, is a favourite with Princess Louise.

The Gold Pantry is a large room, approached by the necessary iron door and a little dark lobby. Daylight comes through two narrow windows, cut in the thick stone walls. The great cupboards from floor to ceiling, and the immense showcase that fills the centre of the room, are all lined with white, which gives an airy effect, and forms a perfect setting for the glory of the mass of gold.

With a view, perhaps, to reducing this wonderful crowd of objects down to figures, which are understood of the people, you may, perhaps, start forth to separate the centre-pieces from amid clusters of candelabra, a continuous background of gold sconces, beaten or *ciselé*, rose-water dishes, salvers and plaques, or endless piles of gold dinner plates and dishes.

To reach fifty or sixty is quickly done, but then you lose count. You think you have mastered the contents of the case, only to find that on the level of the floor is a huge plateau, bearing on its shining surface several exquisitely modelled groups of figures or animals, each one a perfect centrepiece in itself, while high above your head, and almost out of sight, is a shelf crowded with great flagons, bowls, and tazza shaped dishes.

So you wisely give up your efforts to number the greater glories of the "Gold Pantry" and fall to admiring the principal pieces of the goldsmith's art. Close on your left hand as you enter is the famous "St. George" candelabra. On the broad base the battle between "St. George and the Dragon" is being fought to the death, while the persecuted victim—a beautifully modelled nude female figure—clings to a branch of the twisted oak tree that rears seven candles four feet above the level of the table. In the next case but one, are many large flagons in the shape known as "pilgrim's bottle." Among these is one of exquisite design and workmanship. It was taken from the ship of the Spanish Admiral after the defeat of the Armada. There are also some gold Spanish drinking cups. With but few exceptions (notably a charming round gold dish worked by Cellini), the Spanish flagons and cups are the antiquities of the collection. All the Crown plate was melted down during the civil wars of Charles I.'s reign, and the vast quantity now at Windsor was mainly collected by Anne, George III., and George IV., and the Queen herself. The wonderful gold dinner service for 140 persons, four very large flagons, and a great number of candelabra, were all added by George IV.

The entrée dishes of this service completely fill a large case at the end of the room. They are square in shape, of considerable depth to admit of the heating apparatus, and of great weight. This grand service is supplemented when necessary by thirty dozen gold plates, which are elaborately edged with a chased floral design. The business of giving out this service for use is a most anxious one, and every piece of it is carefully examined before being put away, in case any damage has been done to it.   Close to one of the windows, in a glass case by itself, is the gold font from which all the Queen's children have been christened.   It is tazza shaped and about twenty-four inches high.   Round the base are lovely models of nude children playing small harps.   The edge of the basin is decorated with a thickly twined wreath of lily buds and leaves.   Most interesting are a pair of quaint specimens of Chinese art, in which tinted golds and coloured stones have been worked into the semblance of two flowering shrubs.

More strictly personal, however, to Her Majesty is much of the contents of the enormous glass case that runs the length of the room.   The centre of the case is filled by eleven huge pieces of gold plate, but these are surrounded by objects that are most touching, indicating as they do the Queen's unalienable affection for memorials of her friends.   The end of the case nearest to the door contains a most exquisitely modelled group of " John Brown, Esq.," who leans against the side of a favourite pony, "Flora," and caresses "Sharp," the Queen's pet collie, with his left hand.   This group, which is dated 1869, is flanked by two fine figures of Highlanders, the one " Putting the Stone," the other " Throwing the Hammer."   At the further end of this case, close to a magnificent vase won at Lincoln Races, is a fine statuette in gold of Ross, the " Queen's favourite piper."   A pair of panniered donkeys make pretty salt-cellars.   They came from Nice.   This case also contains four tazza shaped fruit dishes of great value, as well as scores of dainty trifles, and the well-known " Lobster Salt-cellars."

Below is almost a chaos of golden tureens, bowls, and dishes.   The most beautiful of them is a tureen shaped like a nautilus shell. The detail of the base of this tureen is the most marvellous example of goldsmith's work to be seen anywhere. Not far off, though in a different case, is the huge plateau of glass, set in a massive gold frame, on which is the Jubilee gift of the Queen's children and grandchildren.

Beneath the windows are huge fitted cases filled with shallow baize-lined trays. These hold the hundreds of dozens of table implements. Many of these have been added in the present reign, but the knives, forks, and spoons, like those in silver, are of the "shell" pattern. In one window under a small shade is a most formidable-looking knife. It bristles with no fewer than a hundred blades and implements, and was presented to George IV. by the town of Sheffield. On your right hand as you face the windows is a case full of charming inkstands, candlesticks, several handbells (one bearing a bust of Shakespeare), and a thousand and one *bibelots*, many of which have already been described as always being used by Her Majesty in her private apartments.

And now, after glancing curiously at some beautiful snuff boxes, and a few ancient spoons and ladles, you are introduced into the "holy of holies." The passage, which is cut through the very thick stone wall, is lined throughout with cupboards let flush into the wall. Behind the glazed doors nothing is to be seen but a serried mass of gold salt-cellars. There are scores and scores of these, all large and solid, and of several different patterns. The lower parts of these two cases are entirely filled by two enormous oval dishes, each about three feet wide.

Between these golden walls you pass into a rather small room, fitted, like the larger one, with cases from ceiling to ground, and crammed with beautiful objects. Exactly facing the window is a cupboard given up entirely to cups and goblets of a most rare kind.   One large covered mug is encrusted with square rubies and emeralds of immense size and great value.   An exquisite pearl shell is mounted and rimmed in heavy gold, which is covered with diamonds and other gems.

Two carved crystal cups are set in the same costly fashion.   Four nude female figures support an elaborately chased and begemmed goblet, and there are also some ivory carvings in gold settings which form cups fit for a king to drink from.   In all, there are about twenty of these jewelled treasures.

A gold knife, fork, and spoon, the handles of which are encrusted with very fine diamonds, are interesting, being presented to the Queen by the first King of Siam.   Near to them is a huge gold nugget, weighing 328 ounces, sent to Her Majesty from Australia.   A large, square box, marvellously worked in many coloured golds, contained, when it arrived at Windsor, some of the celebrated tributary Cashmere shawls.

Amid a thousand other beautiful things is a fine gold plaque, dated 1671, and bearing the story of the Grecian daughter.   There is also a large silver-mounted flagon, ot Irish bog oak, carved by Lorenez Percy, and depicting scenes at Donnybrook Fair.

Some gold knives and forks set in lovely old china handles are quite delightful, while others, the gold handles of which show scenes from a boar hunt, are massive and very handsome.

The middle of this inner room is filled by the large glass case that shelters one of the most elaborate and wonderful centrepieces among this unique collection.   The design is that of an open Indian temple, wrought and enamelled with a most intricate and delicate pattern, standing on a huge rocky pediment.   Models of three of the Queen's favourite horses in silver are held by Indian servants.

In the centre of the temple is a graceful fountain, which sends forth a tiny jet of Eau-de-Cologne. This scent is poured into the dome of the temple, whence it runs down the supporting pillars and springs from the fountain. The waste runs into the base. The exquisite piece of work was executed some years ago for the Queen by Her Majesty's goldsmiths in the Haymarket. The whole thing is of enormous weight, and, like all the large centrepieces and candelabra, comes to pieces for cleaning or packing purposes.

The value of the Queen's plate is calculated at above three millions of pounds, and incredible as it may seem, the greater part of it is moved to London at least four times a year, namely, on the occasions of the State parties at Buckingham Palace.

It speaks much for the trust placed in the Queen's servants, that there is little or no ceremony or fuss during the carriage of some million pounds' worth of property. No force of police or military escort is told off to guard it. It is passed between the Royal Palaces in so unostentatious a manner that no one is aware of the contents of the big dark *fourgons* that go so quietly through the London streets.

One precaution — and that of the simplest kind — is however always taken. The Royal plate is moved in broad daylight, and at a time when all the world is out and about.

CHAPTER XXIII

THE QUEEN AS A MUSICIAN AND ARTIST

WHEN quite a little child, and yet in the laborious and early stages of acquiring a technical knowledge of music, Princess " Drina " was told by her instructor that without industry and perseverance she would never become mistress of the pianoforte.

" But what would you think of me," cried the high-spirited Princess, " if I became mistress of it in the next minute ? "

" That would be impossible without study.   There is no royal road to music."

" No royal road, eh ?   And I am not mistress of my own piano ? " said Her Royal Highness briskly.   " I will show you that I am, and that *this* is the royalest and easiest road."

With that the Princess shut down the instrument, locked it, and popped the key in her pocket.   " That's being mistress of the piano, and the royal road to learning is, never to take a lesson until you're in the mood for it."

But despite her summary way of treating the art of music, the Queen became in due time a most accomplished performer.   She read music—even the most difficult—with ease and accuracy, played with spirit and excellent

taste, and sang quite delightfully. Besides this, her knowledge and her memory of the greatest standard works is
infallible.

Despite the simplicity of her bringing up, she, even as a
child, was taken frequently to the Opera, and long before
she came to the throne, she knew intimately all the
oratorios from hearing, singing, and playing them. Her
undoubted talent and love for music was first fostered by
her mother, the Duchess of Kent, who was devoted to
music and a fine performer, and subsequently by the
Prince Consort, who was a musician of a very high order
He sang with taste and style, composed exceedingly well,
and was a magnificent organist. The Prince and the
Queen in their early married days were very fond of
dining absolutely alone, and of passing the evening singing duets, with perhaps only a Maid of Honour with them
to play the accompaniments.

In those days, even more than now, when the Queen has
Princess Henry of Battenberg and so many of her grand-
daughters to play for her, the Maids of Honour had to be
very clever musicians. One or other was for ever being
sent for to try over new music, play duets with Her
Majesty, or accompany the Prince Consort. Almost the
first popularity won by the Liddell family at Court in
George IV.'s time was insured by their extraordinary
talent for music, and by the very lovely voices most of
them possessed. The three elder Misses Liddell, who
afterwards became Lady Hardwicke, Lady Barrington, and
Lady Williamson, often sang to the " First Gentleman in
Europe." Lady Normanby, another of the family, became
Lady-in-Waiting to the Queen on her accession. It was
she who one day took her youngest sister, a very charming
musician, to sing before the Queen.

In fear and trembling the young girl sang a famous

operatic *scena*, which was one of Grisi's great airs, but omitted the shake at the end. Her Majesty, who knew accurately every opera then in vogue, said: "Does not your sister shake, Lady Normanby?" Her Ladyship smartly replied: "Oh! yes, ma'am, she is shaking all over"; at which the Queen was vastly entertained.

Shake or no shake, this same young lady soon afterwards became a very dear and devoted Maid of Honour to the Queen. Her Majesty was very partial to pianoforte performances *à quatre mains*. She played all Beethoven's greatest works this way, and all the most difficult Masses as duets. Frequently Michael Costa, the famous conductor, would be commanded either to Windsor or Buckingham Palace, to accompany Her Majesty or to practise with her and give her hints on the great operatic *scenas* which at that time it was so fashionable for amateurs to sing.

The Queen can lay claim to having been one of the few who ever understood the marvellously intricate score of Spohr's "Creation of Sound," which the celebrated orchestra of the Philharmonic were unable to learn correctly till Spohr himself came over and explained it to the musicians.

In fact, much of the Queen's spare time was given up to the thoughtful study and steady practising of classical music, which nowadays young women condemn as being "too dull and too difficult." She frequently sang through the whole of great works with her ladies, and a "Miserere" of Costa's found much favour with her, and was often rendered by her and those about her who were musical.

The Queen's first visit to Scotland, in 1842, made her intimately acquainted with the bagpipes. She was much pleased with them at Taymouth Castle, and ever since then a piper has played within her hearing during breakfast time.

Ross, of whom the Queen possesses a beautiful statuette in solid gold, was for years her favourite piper.

Campbell was another fine performer, whose duty it was to play beneath the Queen's windows early in the morning.

One of the prettiest incidents connected with the musical side of the Queen's life was her delightfully frank and unaffected friendship with that sweetest of musicians, Mendelssohn. He often went to the Palace to see Prince Albert, and his last visit there was singularly pleasant.

"Prince Albert had asked me to go to him on Saturday at two o'clock so that I might try his organ before I left England. I found him alone, and as we were talking away, the Queen came in, also alone, and in a simple morning dress. She said she was obliged to leave for Claremont in an hour, and then, suddenly interrupting herself, exclaimed : ' But goodness, what a confusion ! ' for the wind had littered the whole room, and even the pedals of the organ (which, by the way, made a very pretty feature in the room) with leaves of music from a large portfolio that lay open. As she spoke she knelt down and began picking up the music ; Prince Albert helped, and I too was not idle. Then Prince Albert proceeded to explain the stops to me, and she said that she would meanwhile put things straight. I began my chorus from ' St. Paul ' : ' How lovely are the messengers.' Before I got to the end of the first verse they both joined in the chorus. Then the young Queen asked if I had written any new songs, and said she was very fond of singing my published ones. ' You should sing one to him,' said Prince Albert ; and after a little persuasion, she said she would try the ' Frühlingslied ' in B flat. The song could not, however, be found, and she offered to sing one of Glück's. Eventually, a volume of Mendelssohn's songs was discovered, and the Queen chose " Schöner und schöner schmuckt sich.' She sang it quite charmingly, in strict time and tune, and with very good execution. Only in the line, ' Der Prosa Lasten und Mith,' where it goes down to D and then comes up again by semi-tones, she sang D sharp each time, and I gave her the note the two first times. The last time she sang D where it ought to have been D sharp. But with the exception of this little mistake it was really charming, and the last long G I have never heard better or purer, or more natural from any amateur."

The Queen's admiration for Jenny Lind was of the very highest, and her appreciation for her both as a singer and actress was unbounded. She always spoke of the famous cantatrice as "quite a remarkable phenomenon," and of " the purity of her singing and acting as indescribable."

The great Lablache, who had taught Her Majesty to sing, was also a fervent admirer of Lind's, and he and the Queen spent many hours in talking over and going through her various performances.

The Queen had a perfect passion for operatic perform-ances, *Fidelio*, *Les Huguenots*, *Don Giovanni*, *Il Flauto Magico*, and *Le Prophète* were the operas generally com-manded for State performances. On other occasions the works of Rossini, Auber, and Donizetti have afforded the Queen infinite pleasure.

One of the most magnificent gala performances the Queen ever attended was given at Her Majesty's Theatre in 1855 when the Emperor Napoleon III. and the Empress Eugénie were paying a State visit to this country. The opera given was *Fidelio*. It was during the Crimean War, and the Emperor of the French was much struck by the peculiar fact that the entwined initials of the four Royal names, N. E. V. A., spelt Neva, and remarked on this to the Queen.

Her Majesty's own talent for art has always made her very warm-hearted towards those who practise music as a profession. She entertained a sincere admiration for Sir Michael Costa, Lablache, and for Mrs. Anderson, her own and her childrens' music-mistress. It was "Andy" who was present—giving a music lesson to one of the younger Princesses—when the Princess Royal, in the act of sending a letter to her *fiancé*, the Crown Prince Frederick of Prussia, caught the muslin sleeve of her gown alight and was severely burned on the right arm. Mrs. Anderson's husband the Master of the Queen's private band, was of great assistance to Her Majesty at the time the splendid new organs were selected and built up in St. George's Hall, Windsor, and in the New Concert Hall, Buckingham Palace.

Since those lights of other days have faded out, the Queen has admitted Madame Albani to a near friendship. She frequently sends for her to Court, and dearly loves to hear her sing the ballads and *arias* that were popular fifty years ago. At the same time Her Majesty is not averse to more modern music. She has derived immense pleasure from *Faust*, while of *Carmen* she is quite fond. Many of Sir Arthur Sullivan's light operas she also likes, but Wagner has found little or no favour with the Queen.

Other musicians whom the Sovereign liked to have about her were Signor Tosti, who, until the Duchess' death, used to go for an hour every evening to St. James's Palace and sing and play to the aged Duchess of Cambridge ; and also Miss Jessie Ferrari, the clever daughter of an able father. Miss Ferrari taught Princess Henry of Battenberg to sing, and when the Court is at Windsor is always a frequent visitor to the Queen's private apartments. Here, until recently, she accompanied the Queen in her singing and played duets with her.

Every piece of music, that is worthy of the name, is always sent to the Queen, who listens and criticises, while Princess Henry—who is a fine pianist and organist—or a Maid of Honour plays and sings.

The Queen's taste in music is excellent, while her knowledge enables her to sift the imitation from the original. Mere noise and tuneless vapourings have, however, never found favour with Her Majesty.

It is scarcely the Queen's fault that her education and training in painting should not have been of so exceedingly high an order as her cultivation in music.

The great masters of colour and form were all dead at the time the Queen's teaching began, and for over half a century none arose to fill their vacant places. · Yet that as a child she must have had considerable taste in pictorial art is shown by the delicate sketch of a girl she made under the direction of her drawing master, Westall, in her tenth year, and which she gave on his last birthday to her uncle, George IV. During her girlhood she also made a number of most delightful drawings and sketches, many of them showing a great feeling for humour.

It was noticeable that after her marriage her taste and style in drawing altered. Prince Albert was himself an excellent artist and faithful delineator, and many of his works in pencil, crayon, and colour, that hang in the Queen's private rooms, are charming. But an element of Teutonism flavoured all his pictorial work, and under his guidance Her Majesty lost some of the freedom and ease of her style.

Early in her married life, the Queen and Prince Consort, under the tutilage of Thomas Landseer, R.A., a brother of Sir Edwin Landseer, and an able etcher, took up etching, and amused themselves by reproducing their own and each other's drawing of their children and pet animals. The

THE QUEEN'S DRAWING-ROOM AT OSBORNE.

little etchings which, though small and slight, were exceedingly clever, and impressions from the plates of the Royal artists were highly prized by those fortunate friends to whom they were sometimes presented. At the same time the Queen had a strenuous objection to any of her work being exhibited or in any way made public.

A great scandal ensued therefore when in 1848 a man called Jasper Tomsett Judge, who had been picking up a living in Windsor as a journalist, announced an Exhibition of some fifty or sixty etchings by the Queen and Prince Consort, and went so far as to circulate a catalogue of the pictures. Her Majesty was greatly annoyed, and the fellow was only stayed by an injunction obtained in the High Courts, on affidavits sworn by Prince Albert and by Mr. Brown, the Queen's printer at Windsor, who had been entrusted with the printing of the etchings, and from whose works a dishonest printer had stolen the impressions.

Three or four years ago a portfolio of etchings was sold in Dublin for a few shillings that proved to be the work of the Queen and Prince Albert. They were those that the Queen had once given to her friend, Lady Charlemont.

The Queen's choice of foreign portrait painters to perpetuate her own and her relations' features has been canvassed for years. As a matter of fact, Her Majesty was forced by lack of native talent to patronise the Winter-halters, and Professor von Angeli. The habit once contracted has not been entirely broken through, though Her Majesty possesses scores of portraits and pictures by Englishmen and Scotchmen, and has herself often sat to English painters.

Whenever it was possible the Queen gave commissions to her own subjects. A beautiful summer-house in the grounds of Buckingham Palace was, in 1843, decorated with eight fine panels in fresco, and the artists chosen to paint these pictures, which illustrated Milton's "Comus," were Sir Edwin Landseer, Sir William Ross, Dyce, Eastlake, Maclise, Leslie, Stanfield, and Uwins. The Queen watched the work with the deepest interest, and would frequently indicate an effect she wished produced.

At Windsor, almost all the leading modern painters are represented, and Her Majesty had an unfeigned admiration for the talents of the late Sir Frederick Leighton and the late Sir John Millais.

Of sketching, the Queen was till recently very fond, and she never started on the shortest of walks or pony-back rides without her sketch-book. In this simple fashion the Queen has accumulated a vast store of memorials of every place she has ever visited. Her attempts at portraiture are excellent. Many of her faithful gillies and maids have been her sitters.

In clay the Queen at one time showed very considerable talent, and it has always been a matter of regret that such a decided ability for modelling as she undoubtedly possessed should, for absolute lack of time, have been perforce neglected.

Her great artistic feelings and her extraordinary capacities for performance have been transmitted to most of her children. The Empress Frederick is a very good painter indeed, and a beautiful pianist. The Duke of Coburg's capabilities with the violin are as well known as are Princess Louise's with the mallet and chisel. The late Duke of Albany was a splendid musician, and composed a great deal, and Princess Henry of Battenberg sketches, acts, composes, sings, and plays.

CHAPTER XXIV

THE QUEEN'S PRIVATE HOUSES

Osborne

THERE is no doubt that the happiest hours of the Queen's long and glorious reign have been spent in the quiet country retreats she, by wise economy and care, was able to purchase for herself, and amid the simple sanctity of family life. When all is said and done, Her Majesty is but flesh and blood, nerves and heart, like the humblest and most irresponsible of her subjects, and it must at times have been nothing but the short intervals of repose she was able to snatch at Balmoral or Osborne which enabled her to bear with such grand courage and wonderful self-restraint the heat and burden of that long day which is, even yet, not finished.

Very soon after the Queen's marriage, she made up her mind that she must have some home of her very own, where, beneath the shade of clustering trees, and accompanied only by the song of birds, Her Majesty could cast aside the splendour of Court life, forget for a time Prime Ministers and Privy Councils, and give full vent to that tender love for her husband and that maternal solicitude for her young family which have been the two most beautiful traits in a character ever " pure womanly."

Before everything, the young Queen, whose training as a child had been entirely domestic, and the Prince Consort had the most simple of tastes, while their affection and appreciation of Nature's fairest works was both mutual and genuine. But greatly as they admired and enhanced the beauties of Royal Windsor, the Queen and the Prince could never forget that the great country retreat of kings and courtiers was regulated by Public Departments which reduced life there to the semblance of a vast hotel instead of a "home," the love of which is so strongly imbued in those who have English or German blood in their veins. Her Majesty soon made her feelings on this important subject known among the more intimate members of her immediate circle. She wished to buy Norris Castle, but the price asked was in her mind prohibitive. It was on Sir Robert Peel, whom by that time the Queen had come to regard as a tried friend and most trusty servant, that the honour fell of first bringing the estate of Osborne in the Isle of Wight before the notice of the Queen and her husband. Its recommendations were many. It was not too far removed from London and the various Governmental offices, yet it was so retired, in fact almost unknown to the majority of people, that among its shady walks and leafy groves the Queen would easily obtain the privacy and retirement she so ardently longed for. The bathing and boating in the vicinity were excellent, and the panoramic views across the Solent to Portsmouth, and the great roadstead of Spithead and farther down the Channel to where the swelling downs of Devonshire rose palely through the summer mists made the little spot an ideal marine home to replace the Pavilion at Brighton, which her Majesty disliked so intensely.

On Sir Robert Peel's recommendation, therefore, Osborne House and the adjacent grounds, covering some eight hundred acres, were bought from Lady Isabella Blatchford, the purchase being completed on the 25th March, 1844.   It was soon found, however, that the existing mansion house was totally inadequate to the requirements of the Queen, her household, and a rapidly increasing family.   It was at once pulled down, and on the 23rd of June, 1844, the Royal couple laid the first stone of what was afterwards destined to be the happiest and most favoured of their houses.   So determined were the Queen and the Prince Consort that Osborne should be their own, in creation as well as in possession, that the Prince himself planned and designed the house, subject always to the approval of the Queen and to the technical advice of Mr. Thomas Cubitt, for whose opinions the Prince had sincere respect.

Osborne House, as the Prince Consort designed and knew it, took six years to build, although the pavilion at the north-west end of the pile, where are situated the Royal apartments and the nurseries, was pushed forward and completed within a year.   Prince Albert and Mr. Toward, the land steward of Osborne, under him, were also some five years in laying out and re-arranging to the fullest advantage the lovely grounds, which have more than repaid the time, trouble, and money expended on them.   Since that time, Osborne House and its environs have been considerably enlarged.   A new wing, the wonderful Indian Room, and the Private Chapel, or Prayer Room, as it is called, have been added to the mansion itself, while the manor and farms of Barton, various cottages with their grounds, and much woodland have increased Her Majesty's holding in the Isle of Wight to five thousand acres, extending the property by the seashore to within a very short distance of Ryde, while inland the celebrated Osborne preserves impinge nearly upon Newport.   When the Queen first acquired her delightful new toy, she wrote to her uncle Leopold, King of the Belgians, " It sounds so pleasant to have a place of our own, quiet and retired, and free from all Woods and Forests and other charming Departments, which really are the plague of one's life." A few days later she again wrote, " It is impossible to see a prettier place with woods and valleys and points of view which would be beautiful anywhere, but when these are combined with the sea (to which the woods grow down) and a bush which is quite private, it is really everything one could wish."

A charming lodge of freestone, and gates which are jealously boarded up, separate the grounds proper of Osborne House from the road. Once within, a view that is almost tropical in luxuriance of growth and colour of flowers meets the eye. A very fine avenue here starts for the House, but a sharp turn in it is cleverly arranged to obstruct all view of the mansion till the leafy road runs into the straight, when a fine panorama is unfolded.

All around is a most beautiful wood which frames the velvety lawns, the terraces, and gardens of Osborne House. The one break in the green belt is of a brilliant blue and silver. It is the Solent, alive with white-winged yachts and huge steamships, and in its turn bounded by the misty outline of the Hampshire shore. In such a fair setting is the Queen's house proudly set.

The house of freestone is in the Italian style of architecture, judiciously modified to the exigencies of the English climate. It is of pleasantly varied elevation, and has many wings and façades, which lend to the building an air of light picturesqueness, that might not perhaps be considered quite orthodox by sticklers for conventionality as exemplified by English domestic architecture. The features that naturally first catch the eye are the Clock Tower, 90 feet in height, and bearing a clock, the face of which measures 8 feet across, and the Flag Tower, 112 feet high. This latter fine *campanile*, which is at our right hand, rears its graceful outline above the Pavilion, where are situated, on the ground-floor, the dining-room and the Royal billiard-room, adjoining the drawing-room. Above these are the Queen's private sitting-room, overlooking the Solent and the lovely view beyond, and her bed and dressing-rooms. On the top floor are the Royal nurseries, once in the occupation of the Queen's own children, but now given over to the use of H.R.H. Princess Henry of Battenberg, who herself has a fine suite of rooms in the New Wing. The three windows of the Queen's private sitting-room are set in a bay, and may be distinguished from all others by the balcony before, and the green Venetian canopy above them.

On the same level runs a graceful, open colonnade, along which, and without the fatigue of intervening stairs, Her Majesty can travel from her private apartments to the other end of the house, even to the shallow staircase which leads down to the prayer-room at the extreme left.

The entire aspect of the house, the flat roofs and low chimneys inclosed within light balustrades, which are pointed at intervals with gracefully carved urns and vases, all suggest azure skies and southern suns, an effect which is strongly intensified by the marble groups scattered amidst the foliage, the statues standing in niches, and by a chance glimpse of the Queen herself, sitting in the open air, having tea in her favourite seat—the upper alcove. This spot is at the left end of the house, and the daintily spread table and two of the chairs are curiously carved from huge blocks of English coal. From this elevation Her Majesty enjoys in the summer a perfect view of the extraordinary beauties of the Upper and Lower Terraces, the flower-beds of which, cut boldly in the emerald turf, literally blaze with brilliant bloom. The principal features which attract notice are the curiously black hairy stem of a grand China palm, a beautiful model in bronze of " Eos," that graceful

greyhound which was the Prince Consort's constant companion ; a spirited group comprising a chubby boy struggling
with a swan, and mythological figures of winged animals,
slim greyhounds *couchant*, and innumerable tazza-shaped
vases filled with growing flowers, which light up the long
sweeping line of the fretted balustrades.

From the Lower Terrace you must admire the effect of
a charmingly copied Italian *percola*, over which a broad-
leaved vine luxuriates in summer. No prettier sight,
however, can be seen than the pillars swarming with
heavy-headed roses of cream colour, red, and white, while
all around bloom, against their glistening dark leaves,
great masses of crimson and white camellias, and in the
distance sparkling fountains spring from the slender throat
of a bronze swan, and from the half-opened buds of
water lilies.   Guarding a flight of twelve stone steps,
leading from the Upper to the Lower Terrace, are two
noble stone lions.   Standing between them is an alcove
quaintly decorated with cockle shells, and the Valley Walk,
hedged with choice evergreens of many kinds and many
countries, in large square boxes.   They were planted by
various members of the Royal Family, to celebrate, as the
affixed labels indicate, May 24th, 1851.   Here, too, facing
the fountain, is the Lower Alcove, sacred to the Royal
children's tea parties, when the weather is too wet for
these functions to be held on the sea shore or on the
lawn.

A little farther on is a large cypress tree.   It faces the
Solent and is backed by some sheep penned within hurdles.
Here, also, Her Majesty frequently has a fancy, in fine
weather, to drink her tea of an afternoon.

The Queen's entrance to Osborne House is less imposing
than that at Windsor, and scarcely so picturesque as that at
Balmoral.   It lies in a sheltered nook between the two

wings. Before it is a great granite-edged circle, filled with heather from the Scottish moors. The walls of the hall are painted to imitate marble. On the left of the entrance is the Queen's comfortable lift. In the centre of the well of the bright staircase is a large marble group, "The Amazons," and at the foot of the pedestal is a brass gun taken at Tel-el-Kebir and presented to Her Majesty by Lord Alcester in 1882. On the right, facing the first flight of stairs, is a low memorial altar of yellow and green-veined marbles, relieved by ormulu wreaths supporting three busts, the Prince Consort and his two elder sons, which are respectively dated 1871, 1875, and 1879.

On the first floor are the Queen's Private Rooms, consisting of a sitting-room, bed and dressing rooms, and an apartment for the wardrobe women. On the staircase, just above this interesting suite, is a statue of heroic size of the Prince Consort in Roman costume.

Her Majesty's private sitting-room is lofty and large, and almost square in shape, save where the curving bay, which frames the three long windows, breaks the straight lines. It is very light and cheerful, for an unimpeded view across the sea is not veiled with voluminous curtains or shut out by heavy blinds. The impression of the room is one of extreme simplicity and homeliness. The walls, instead of being as at Windsor, panelled in costly silk damask, are plainly painted a pale, restful green. The ceiling is undecorated, save for a large plaster centre ornament, and a very simple cornice, which is composed of the conventional "egg and dart" and "rope" borders, between which runs a light floral scroll. The furniture is upholstered in a very ordinary green and red flowered chintz, of a pattern which has been a favourite with the Queen for many years. The window curtains and valances are of the same material, lined with green silk, and edged with a *pompom* fringe.

The floor is covered with Indian matting of the chessboard pattern. The effect of it all is very fresh and soothing.

The small mantelpiece, framing a highly-polished steel grate, which glows all Christmas through with the beech-log fires the Queen so loves, is of white marble, and severely plain, while there is nothing distinctive about the large square mirror which fills the space above. The clock is square, and supports a well-modelled copy of Johann von Dannecker's "Ariadne and the Panther." To the right and left of it on the broad mantelshelf are four vases containing flowers, some half-dozen *cartes de visite* in frames, a pair of five-light candelabras, and two small white busts. These are somewhat dwarfed by a magnificent head and shoulders in white marble of the late Prince Consort, which stands on a tall pedestal at the left of the fireplace and before which is always laid a chaplet of fresh flowers.

Between the windows and the fireplace are the Queen's two brass-edged writing-tables, which are placed alongside each other and are flanked by two smaller stands. One of these holds the stationery case of black-edged note-paper, stamped very unobtrusively with Her Majesty's cipher, V.R.I.; the other is laden with some dozen books of reference and directories, all bound in green morocco and stamped in gold.

Beneath are tiers holding the correspondence and despatch boxes, which indicate that even in her country house the Queen is never quite free from affairs of State and private business connected with her great fortune and large family. In front of the writing-tables stand two ordinary drawing-room chairs, one of which is redeemed from Spartan simplicity by the large round footstool before it, and a little square cushion suspended across the back by ribbon loops. Above hangs, by three chains, a triple lamp of ormulu and china, which throws a brilliant light by night over a large collection of photographs, miniatures, and statuettes, which are necessary adjuncts to the Queen's writing-tables wherever she may be.

Among the fascinating litter, which would well repay a lengthened examination, places of honour are assigned to a large, full-length likeness of the Prince Consort, and a very sweet picture of the Duchess of Kent set in an oval frame. A large round table near at hand bears, amid a host of minor objects, a huge vase of flowers, which as often as not are from the fields and hedgerows. The grand piano is placed between the left-hand wall and the writing-tables. A bowl of flowers, a pair of candlesticks, shaded with dainty butterflies, and many photographs in plain folding leather frames, are scattered over its broad top. Beneath the keyboard stands a music stool of the old-fashioned "screw" type, which still survives here, though at Windsor, as we have seen, Her Majesty's dislike of change has been overcome in this respect.

There are about fifty pictures on the wall, two-thirds of which are interesting from a purely family point of view, for they are principally portraits, at various ages, of her children, her sons and daughters-in-law, and relations, most of them being from the brushes of the two Winterhalters and H. von Angeli.

To enumerate the many small tables and *etagères*, with their constantly changing burden of books which are being read, art portfolios under inspection, and music in course of being tried over, would be to stamp with perpetuity the only features in the Queen's life which are evanescent.

Her Majesty's bedroom is a large airy apartment by no means overcrowded with furniture, all of which is very homely and substantial, the wardrobes being of mahogany and the chairs and couches covered with the same patterned chintz as in the sitting-room. The walls are painted salmon pink. The most important article of furniture is the Queen's bed, which faces the windows, and, like that at Buckingham Palace, is large and almost square, with a large heavy fringed canopy over the head. Above the pillows is a memorial wreath, beneath which is a framed posthumous portrait of the Prince Consort. Hanging almost in the centre is the bell-rope, and to right and left are two watch-pockets. At the foot of the bed, which is covered with a down quilt, is a large sofa. To the left of the bed is a door, above which hangs Grissi's picture of "Christ Breaking Bread," and immediately about the door the two walls are principally devoted to sacred pictures, the most noticeable among which are "The Madonna and Child," by William Dyce, R.A., and a pencil sketch of Raphael's most beautiful "Virgin and Child." On the right of the bed, hanging above a large chest of drawers, is F. van Eycken's panel "L'Abondance." Next to it is Winterhalter's " Cousins," and above the fire-place a large picture by G. Yager of "The Entombment of Christ."

The mantelpiece itself is of white marble, with a very narrow shelf on which are ranged eight small busts, in the centre of which stands a carriage clock. To the right and left of the hearth are a portrait of the Prince Consort in armour, and a large tapestry screen.

The toilette appliances at Osborne are pretty, but very simple in design and pattern.

The dining-room which invariably is used by Her Majesty is a commodious apartment looking south-east over the Upper Terrace towards the Clock Tower and the Vinery. The big bay-window faces the green marble mantelpiece and sheds ample light on a handsome clock and pair of bronzes by Deniére, of Bruges, and two quaint vases, illustrating the fable of "The Fox and the Stork." The room is furnished entirely in mahogany, and contains, in addition to a round table and a veritable crowd of chairs, five full-sized sideboards and an old-fashioned wine-cooler, all supported on feet formed of winged lions.

At the far end from the door is the beautiful Winterhalter, showing the Prince Consort in Court dress with the Queen and their first five children. Another really delightful picture is that painted in 1844 of the Duchess of Kent. It shows her as a sweet-faced old lady in a poke bonnet, walking down a country lane, and is full of atmosphere and colour. Princess Beatrice in 1863, by Lambert, wears half-mourning for her father, whose miniature she holds in her hand. A large picture of the late Emperor of Germany and the Empress Frederick with their children, represents the present Emperor wearing an ample blue sash, and Prince Henry of Prussia in a pink cap and holding a coral and bells. Princess Louise with the Princes Arthur and Leopold are in a picture by Winterhalter, painted in 1850; and there are family groups of the Grand Duke and Grand Duchess of Hesse, and the Prince and Princess of Wales with Prince Eddie in a Scotch kilt.

The Drawing-room is a truly delightful apartment with a large bay-window looking on to the East Terrace. The walls are distempered in a cool shade of blue; the doors are painted in white and gold; and the ceiling, like that in the Billiard-room, is Pompeian in decoration. Amid such surroundings, the innumerable pictures and the amber-covered damask furniture show to extreme advantage. The grand piano and the wall cabinets are of tulip wood, inlaid in plaques of Wedgwood jasper ware mounted in ormulu. The mantelpiece is of plain white marble, and is surmounted by a French clock in gilt and bronze, and four good specimens of ivory and ormulu work. It is flanked at either side by two vases of immense value. They are of glass and gold, are five feet high, and, as a rule, are hidden behind the doors of the cabinets which contain them. A dainty white screen with eight brackets decorated with gold, stands always before the fire. The chandeliers of brilliant cut glass, hang from the ceiling, and are always filled with wax candles. Two pillars of glass, eight feet high, which stand on either side of the bay-window, sometimes support oil lamps. A characteristic break is made in the wall decoration by six cabinets full of books of many nations and all kinds. Among them figure *Pearson's Magazine*, Brontë's and Dickens' works, " Mountain, Loch, and Glen," and the " Vicar of Wakefield " in French. Most of the books are in the Queen's favourite binding of dark green morocco, and have her cipher in the centre of the cover.

Running at right angles with the Drawing-room, and only separated from it by handsome pillars, is the Billiard-room, a magnificent apartment, which, like the Grand Corridor that runs through the house from end to end, contains a quantity of striking statuary.

Landseer's most famous picture, " The Deer Pass," hangs in the Council-room, a beautiful apartment overlooking the Upper Terrace. The Indian Room, with its exquisite carvings and fairy-like sense of whiteness, is well-known to the public through the medium of the illustrated papers. The bedrooms above it have proved a valuable addition to the accommodation of Osborne House.

Here in this restful domain the Queen spends many happy hours. There are eight miles of drives on the estate, and the cottages—in reality delightful villas—are occupied by members of the Royal Family and the Court. The bathing in Osborne Bay is excellent and the pheasant shooting at Christmas time is adequate for Her Majesty's guests. In the summer the Queen goes every day to the tennis courts (one of which is asphalted) to watch her children and grandchildren play.

Two charming proofs of the Queen's remembrances for all kinds and conditions of friends are in the Osborne grounds.   One is a granite seat erected in memory of John Brown ; on it is inscribed—

MR. JOHN BROWN,

8th December, 1826.   *27th March*, 1883.

" A truer, nobler, trustier heart, more loving and more loyal, never beat within a human breast."—BYRON.

Behind this is a granite table set squarely in the green turf, on which is written—

WALDMANN.

The very favourite little dachshund of Queen Victoria.
Who brought him from Baden, April, 1872.
Died, July 11th, 1881.

CHAPTER XXV

THE QUEEN'S PRIVATE HOUSES (*continued*)

Balmoral

IT was on September 8th, 1848, that the Queen first saw Balmoral. The estate had been purchased on medical advice as a healthful and restful resort for Her. Majesty, who even then had shown a decided rheumatic tendency. Balmoral is the driest spot in all Scotland, and as such was deemed a suitable residence for the Royal Family. Her Majesty was at once charmed with the little castle, which was of granite, white-washed ("harled" is the Scotch expression), and with many small turrets. The accommodation was, however, very cramped, and it seems impossible to imagine the Queen putting up for so long with such lack of space and comfort. The hall was very small, with a billiard-room and dining-room out of it ; one sitting-room, a bedroom and a "little dressing-room" formed the private suite of the Queen and her husband. The Royal children, with their governess, were lodged in three rooms. The ladies lived below, and the gentlemen upstairs. The accommodation for the servants was equally poor. So wild and natural was the demesne of Balmoral in those days that on the very evening of the Queen's first arrival there the red deer came down to feed quite close to the house.

In September, 1853, the Queen, amid her tenantry and without any great show, laid the foundation stone of the new house. It is of light granite, in the old Scotch Baronial style. The handsome tower that tops it is 100 feet high, while many smaller turrets break the outline agreeably. The Dee runs right under the Castle windows, and, indeed, the whole building has been arranged and constructed to catch all the finest views and the fairest weather. The Prince Consort took the greatest pains with the Balmoral gardens, preferring rather to re-arrange Nature's handiwork, than to replace it by merely artificial devices. The result is admirable, for though flowers bloom rather late in those parts, the foliage of the evergreens and trees is glorious. The splendid arborial growth is so managed that every drive and walk is well sheltered from the cold winds.

In the West Garden stands the Eagle Fountain, given to the Queen by William I. of Germany, when still King of Prussia. Round one angle of the Castle is a beautiful little pleasance, encircled with a dense shrubbery. Here in very fine weather Her Majesty breakfasts and transacts her morning business. At other times she goes straight from her private apartments to a charming cottage, near the house, where she spends the morning hours. It was originally designed for a gardener's use, but Her Majesty so liked it that it was transmogrified for her. It is, like so many Scotch cottages, built of pine-wood and plaster, and contains three rooms. The writing-room is hung entirely with the Balmoral tartan, a plaid of grey and red designed by Prince Albert, and quite distinct from the Victoria tartan, in which there is a large admixture of white. It is this same room, which is so arranged that on fine days one end of it can be thrown open, so that the Queen can get all the air without risk of damp or draught.

The interior of Balmoral Castle is extremely simple—

even homely—and in many eyes seems to lack diversity of colour. Nearly everywhere, save in some of the bedrooms, which are papered, the walls are painted in the pale, cold tints which were so fashionable in the '50's. Except in the Queen's private rooms and in the drawing-room, where hang several water-colour sketches from the brushes of the Royal Family, engravings and photographs form the pictorial decoration. There are stags' heads everywhere, and in the big flagged entrance hall, which is used by Her Majesty, is a boar's head, once belonging to an animal shot by the Prince Consort in Germany. A life-size statue of the Prince, in Highland dress, by Theed, stands in an alcove of the hall. The corridor, which goes through the house, is quite lined with busts, among them being likenesses of the late Emperor Frederick, and the late Dukes of Albany and Hesse, Dr. Norman Macleod, and other faithful servants of the Queen. In fact, Balmoral, more than any other of Her Majesty's houses, breathes almost exclusively of the past, and for its Royal owner must be a house of memories.

The Drawing-room is quaintly old-world, and exceedingly comfortable. Over the floor of square pine blocks is laid a carpet of the Royal Stuart tartan, while the furniture is upholstered with, and the curtains are made from, Victoria tartan. Many tables, a fine grand piano, and a profusion of large chairs are conspicuous in the apartment. That the Queen likes the Stuart tartan is evinced by the fact that it is used as the carpet pattern laid in most of the bedrooms at Balmoral.

Her Majesty, when in her Highland home, generally lunches and dines in the Library. It is under her private apartments, and looks on to the Terrace. It is quite small, and about nine people only can find room at the table. A few of the Queen's favourite books justify the name of the room, which also contains ample sideboards. Strips of

crumb cloth on the floor round the table indicate a truly
Scotch carefulness, and a desire to save the carpet from the
wear of the footmen's tread.

The Household, as a rule, use the Dining-room of the
Castle. It is entered from the corridor that leads to the
Equerries' entrance. It is very plainly furnished, but con-
tains a few interesting engravings—early portraits of the
Queen and Prince Albert, and one of the Queen on pony-
back, after her widowhood.

The big Ball-room is a fine place built of pine, and hung
with tartan. Here all the theatrical performances ever given
at Balmoral have taken place, but as a rule the little concerts
of which Her Majesty is so fond are held quite unostentatiously in the Drawing-room. About these concerts it is
the custom of the Queen's Scotch neighbours to consult
Her Majesty's wishes, and to "put up" among themselves
such artists as she may wish to hear. With her dear friend,
Madame Albani, staying at Mar, and certain singers and
violinists and pianists visiting at houses near by, a charming
concert is easily and frequently arranged and much enjoyed
by Her Majesty. A shallow double staircase into the Ball-
room connects the apartments with the Queen's private
suite. In the winter, unless the Court is in mourning,
the Queen's Factor bids all the tenants and employés,
in Her Majesty's name, to a big ball in this splendid
apartment.

The Service-room, where in later years the Queen has
chosen to worship on Sundays, is very plain, the walls being
of dark Balloch Buie pinewood and the furniture seated with
dark leather. Princess Henry of Battenberg generally plays
a small organ. The service here is always Presbyterian, and
the Queen communicates in the Scotch fashion, even as she
used to do in the little kirk at Crathie, when two long,
narrow tables, covered with white linen, were placed the full

length of the building, and all those who could sit together at them communicated at the same time. The Queen has been but little to Crathie the last few years, for she was driven from her quiet worship there, as she was from the pretty church at Whippingham, by crowds of vulgar and noisy sightseers. Almost the last time that Her Majesty partook of the Holy Communion there, she was much shocked and annoyed by the conduct of a woman, who, after joining in the Sacrament with the Queen (as she was free to do), stood in the aisle and swept an obtrusive courtesy as Her Majesty walked quietly back to her pew in the gallery.

The great features of Balmoral are the Shiels and the Cairns. Of the Shiels, or " bothies," there are four. The nearest to the Castle is the Queen's Shiel, then comes the Danzig Shiel, the Glassalt Shiel, and that favourite retreat of all, the Shiel of Alt-na-guithasach, where the Queen and Prince Consort, with one lady and a few servants, would go every year for some days' real retirement. All are lined with pinewood and upholstered with tartan, a few pairs of antlers and some photos and engravings forming the homely decoration.

Of cairns, a truly Scotch institution, there are many. Each child of the Queen has one, and every marriage or death is identically commemorated. Other memorials at Balmoral include a lovely cross of grey granite to the memory of Princess Alice. The well-known bronze statue of Prince Albert in Highland costume, and with a hound at his side, stands on a rough granite base on the eastern side of the Castle.

It is here, at the foot of this memorial, that on every recurring 26th of August (the lamented Prince's birthday) the Queen, with her family and Court, her servants and tenantry, meet together, amid the most impressive silence, and with bared heads, drink to the memory of the dead.

Nearly opposite this statue is the bronze figure of the Queen, presented to her by her Scotch tenantry in the Jubilee year. Not far off, and amid charming flower-beds, is an obelisk to Prince Albert's memory. There is also a statue of Mr. John Brown.

One of the Queen's favourite morning drives in her chair is along a shady forest road on the east side of Craig Gowan. Here is a memorial seat of fine grey granite, dedicated to Prince Leopold, who died in 1884. In winter, this is carefully boxed in, to keep it from frost.

It is at Balmoral that the Queen is most at home. In every cottage and hut for miles round she is regarded as a personal friend, for in her hours of leisure she has made the sorrow and joys of her people her own. Everybody can point to a " gift " from the Queen, many, indeed, owe everything they possess to this most ideal " Lady Bountiful."

The list of the Queen's private houses is not limited to Osborne and Balmoral. Claremont, Abergeldie Castle and Manse, Frogmore and others are hers. But they are merely incidental, and not material to her private life, and do not bear upon them the impress of Her Majesty's strong personality.

CHAPTER XXVI

THE QUEEN AS A WORKER

THERE is, perhaps, no better definition of the difference between work and play than that contained in Mark Twain's inimitable incident in which the boys come and jeer at Tom Sawyer, whose aunt has sent him to whitewash the fence. The more they jeer, the harder Tom works, and at last he jeers back at them for supposing he is working. He laughs at their insinuation that he has to do the whitewashing. He is only, he tells them, doing it for fun—he hasn't got to do it. The result is that one by one the boys take off their coats and fall to playing the new game of whitewashing the fence.

No doubt most of my readers would think it fine fun to be the Queen, and would take great pleasure in doing her work instead of their own, but it would be a very different story if they had got to do it; but, as they have not, it is not very easy to give an idea of the enormous amount of hard work Her Majesty has to perform. It may be as well therefore to commence by giving a few figures which may enable the reader, if he will keep them in his head, to realise that the following account is not a record of pleasure, but downright hard work, which no City clerk or typewriter in a commercial house after the first week would undertake for any salary you could offer him, to say nothing of doing it every day, without a single regular holiday, for fifty years.

In 1848, for instance, 28,000 despatches were sent from and received at the Foreign Office. Every one of these was closely studied, discussed, advised on, as well as annotated by the Queen. It must be remembered that an equal number emanated from the Home and Colonial Offices. This is over an average of 230 a day, and of course there were other things to do as well. A special Act of Parliament had to be passed in 1862 to slightly mitigate the Sovereign's labour in signing commissions for the Army and Navy, as in that year it was found the Queen was still signing commissions which, since 1854, had got 16,000 in arrears.

It may be said that these figures do not represent a normal time in the life of Her Majesty. The answer to this is, that week in, week out, the work of the Sovereign is pretty much the same, and has been since as a girl of eighteen she came to the throne.

Any lines written of the Queen as a worker must of necessity be somewhat a *résumé* of those various phases of her everyday life which are mentioned in fuller details in this work. Yet it may not be without interest to collect and review them. No greater delusion exists than that the Queen at any period of her life ever indulged herself in idleness, or even in that modified form of " doing nothing " that is more charitably called leisure. Her surroundings and all the influence that was brought to bear on her from her baby days upwards urged her on to work, work, work. During the extreme delicacy of her early girlhood, when it was rumoured that the little Princess " Drina " (as she chose to call herself) would never live to grow up ; during the many enforced retirements of her married life ; during the first sad years of her widow-hood and the many terrible domestic griefs she had endured since, Her Majesty's one watchword has been "work." That it has been no empty phrase is well known by her Ministers, her family, and her Household.

There is no doubt that at the time of the Queen's birth, her mother, the Duchess of Kent, felt very strongly the responsibility of having given birth to one who stood so nearly an heir to the throne. Thus it was that almost from the beginning the child was taught habits of hard work, methods of self-government. When the Princess was only four years old her grandmother, the Dowager Duchess of Coburg, wrote to the Duchess of Kent that one so young should not be forced to acquire book-learning, but the little girl's lessons and strictly methodical mode of life were scarcely mitigated. When still quite tiny she could speak both German and English perfectly, and had acquired a thorough foundation of French, Italian, and Latin.

The usual "ladylike" curriculum of studies of the first quarter of the century was carefully laid down for the Princess. History proved her favourite lesson, and with intuitive quickness she studied the history of her grand-father's long reign and was for ever seeking information as to the political and social improvements that had occurred during that lengthened period. Almost exclusively under the watchful eyes of her mother and the Baroness Lehzen, who conducted her general education, and was always present at the music lessons of Mrs. Anderson and during the discourses of the famous divine, William Wilberforce, to whom was confided the religious instruction of the young Princess, the future Queen was brought up without the faintest knowledge of what her position was to be.

Sir Walter Scott, who met the little girl when dining with the Duchess of Kent, speaks of her as being beautifully educated, and so modest and simple that no one would guess at her rank and prospective condition. Yet the Wizard of the North insinuates that "some pigeon or other birds of the air had carried the matter."

How wrong was his suspicion, and how innocent was the Princess, was afterwards shown by Baroness Lehzen who, in a letter to the Queen in 1867, recalls the whole circumstances of how the knowledge of her true position came to the young girl only six years before she ascended the throne.

From that moment the Princess of her own accord drew up a strict line of life to which she rigidly adhered until that momentous day in 1837 placed her on the throne. Within a few hours of hearing the news of her accession she read an address to her Privy Council with the utmost dignity and composure, and from that hour this young girl of eighteen was plunged into a sea of responsibility, duty, and hard work that might well tax the nerves and health of the strongest man. She at once instituted a habit of early rising, and by the time she was ready to receive her mother at nine o'clock breakfast she had already done an hour's work. Frequently during her married life, when business pressed and her hours for outdoor exercise were curtailed, she would ride at six o'clock for an hour before beginning the day's work.

The reading of the leading papers, English and foreign, of despatches and reports, occupied her until midday, when she always had an audience of her Ministers which was frequently followed by a Privy Council. Every paper and question has always been perused and criticised by the Queen herself, who in her most high-spirited moments has never permitted the slightest deviation from the hard and fast lines of the business in hand which she had to do herself, because the law would not allow a private secretary.

A ride or a drive formed the Queen's only relaxation in those days, for her appearance at Ascot Races, the opera, and theatre, partook more of the nature of duty to the public than pleasure.

The question of her marriage soon added to her daily cares, but it is related of her by one who was present that she settled the matter for herself with the same quiet dignity that distinguished all her other actions. She announced her betrothal herself to the Privy Council attired in a plain morning gown, but wearing a bracelet containing Prince Albert's picture. She read the declaration in a clear, sonorous, sweet-toned voice, but her hands trembled so excessively that it was wonderful she was able to read the paper which she held.

After her marriage, the Queen, so far from drifting into a leisure which would, under the circumstances, have been excusable, worked harder than ever. Prince Albert was devoted to music, and to please him she daily made time to practice both her singing and playing. Her almost endless troubles as a housekeeper I have only space to again refer to, and all the household reforms instituted by the Prince added to her labours, as they were investigated by Her Majesty down to the humblest detail. The vast alterations and improvements made at Windsor Castle and Buckingham Palace were all carried out under her own eye and she often had to find time to inspect the various Royal residences at Hampton, Kew, and Richmond. No day, however long and fatiguing, passed without full entries and most astute comment on passing events being made in the Queen's diary by her own hand, or without her writing a great number of lengthy letters to all members of her family on every conceivable subject of private interest. Yet these were but adjuncts to a life given up to the service of the State and came as relaxations to a mind filled with every minute detail of Home and Foreign policy. It is not my wish to dip into history, but I must give some examples.

In the '40's Her Majesty was filled with anxiety concerning the bad condition of English trade, and she found time to plan and carry out many entertainments and projects to mitigate the friction in the labour market and to alleviate the wide-spread distress. In the '50's the Indian Mutiny, and subsequently the Crimean War, laid fresh burdens on her already over-weighted shoulders. And yet never for one hour, either for reasons of sickness or pleasure, sorrow or indolence, has the Queen failed to face or carry through the overwhelming duties of her worker's life. And this, too, at a period when she was bearing and bringing up a large family of children.

The immense amount of political work entailed by the Crimean War already referred to, and simultaneous home troubles, did not prevent the Queen from exercising her more feminine talents, and after Florence Nightingale went out with thirty-six other lady nurses to Scutari, the Queen daily summoned her friends and Household to sit with her to make every kind of wrap and garment for her sick and dying soldiers.

Once when the Queen was in very delicate health, she was yachting on the Irish coast, under the most trying circumstances of stormy weather and its attendant discomforts. Yet for many hours a day, the Queen sat in the little cabin, reading, signing, and commenting on government affairs, attending to every detail in the vast machinery of her great kingdom, and neither for weather nor ill health leaving one single duty unperformed.

But not only is the Queen's work very hard, it is sometimes very painful, as may be imagined from the following story, and is accompanied by long sleepless nights, the result of over-wrought nerves.

Once the Duke of Wellington brought her a death-warrant to sign, the soldier being an incorrigible deserter. The Queen evinced extreme reluctance to affix her signature, and pressed the Duke for some reason for clemency. At length the Duke admitted that the condemned man had always earned the affection of his fellow-soldiers. The Queen, with tears in her eyes, cried: "Oh, your Grace, I am *so* pleased to hear that," and hastily wrote "Pardoned, Victoria R." across the slip of paper.

But for a strong sense of duty, the Queen would always grant a reprieve, especially in the case of women, for it is easy to imagine the horror her refined nature feels in even indirectly being the cause of any one's death, and it has long been said that the hour of any man's hanging finds the Queen on her knees praying for his soul.

When the condition of the Court of the Regent and George IV. is remembered, it should not be forgotten that the present high standard of honour, virtue, and true goodness that prevails within the Queen's Palaces is entirely due to hard and very disagreeable work, and the strictest personal supervision which the cleaning and keeping clean of the Royal Augean stable necessitates. Even nowadays Her Majesty finds time and energy to overlook the Lord Chamberlain's lists and, if need be, to cut them down. The new regulations for the Drawing-rooms, which have now been in operation for three years, were due entirely to the Queen's own action.

A glance at the COURT CIRCULAR any time during the present reign gives no idea of the labour that is crowded into the Queen's waking hours. When the world reads of the Queen driving out it naturally supposes that she is lolling in a carriage doing nothing. Those about her, however, know that she is more often than not making a tour of inspection among her farms, through the scores of glass fruit, and flower houses, round the stables, dairies, or kennels, and inquiring after the comfort and welfare of her retainers. All these various affairs the Queen manages herself with the same amount of care and thoroughness that mark her consideration of an important debate and reply to a question of International policy.

For many years past the Queen's health and strength have largely depended on her being almost perpetually in the open air, and it is necessity rather than choice that obliges her to do all her morning's work out of doors. At Windsor the little Frogmore tea house, with its lovely surroundings, is the chosen spot, and here, beneath the shade of two magnificent evergreen oaks, the Queen's writing-table and despatch boxes are set out on fine mornings, while two mounted messengers keep up perpetual communication with the telegraph office and telephones at the Castle, and the attendant secretary stands at her side.

The routine of the messengers when the Court is at Balmoral is much the same as when Her Majesty is on the Continent, allowing, of course, for a difference in the length of the journeys. The messengers who are despatched alternately by the Home Office, the Foreign Office, and the Lord Chamberlain's Office, leave London every day, except Sunday, at 2.30 p.m., and travel straight through to Aberdeen, whence a special train starts at 3.50 a.m., landing messengers, parcels, and papers at Ballater about 5 o'clock. Balmoral is reached at 6 o'clock, and all papers are taken to the Private Secretary, who opens and arranges everything in readiness for the Queen's consideration by 10 o'clock, by which time the Minister in Attendance is prepared to go to the Queen when he is sent for. All important papers are ready for the return messenger by 2.30 p.m. and the Queen is then free to discuss and answer her own voluminous correspondence, unless, indeed, very pressing

affairs of State demand further work. At Windsor the
Queen has a double set of messengers going between
the Castle and the heads of the State department in
London, and when there she not infrequently works
before retiring to rest, though this is now done against
the advice of her body physicians. The Osborne posts
and messengers, as the following Official list shows,
leave little leisure even when the Queen is supposed to
be resting.

Osborne.

AUGUST, 1893.

*Arrivals and Departures of Post and Queen's Messengers to and from
London.*

WEEK DAYS.
ARRIVAL.

Morning Post	7.30 and 11 a.m.
Do. Queen's Messenger	4.0 p.m.
Evening Post	6.0 p.m.

DEPARTURES.

Morning Post	8.30 and 12 a.m.
Afternoon, Queen's Messenger	1.30 p.m.
Evening Post	6.0 p.m.
Do. Queen's Letter Bag	8.0 p.m.

ARRIVAL OF FOREIGN MESSENGERS.

In London (Mondays)	About 10 a.m.
At Osborne	4 p.m.

DEPARTURE OF FOREIGN MESSENGERS.

To Germany (Wednesdays)	About 1.30 p.m.
From London	6.45 p.m.

It will be seen that there is little enough time between
times to receive, read, answer and despatch the enormous
amount of correspondence which necessitates all this coming
and going. But on the other side of the card will be found :

SUNDAYS.

ARRIVALS.

Morning Post	7.30 a.m.
Afternoon, Queen's Messenger	3.0 p.m.

DEPARTURES.

Afternoon, Queen's Messenger	4.0 p.m.
Do. Post	6.0 p.m.
Do. Queen's Letter Bag	8.0 p.m.

I will not worry the reader with the times of church and trains and steamboats which this card also supplies, but pass on to other things.

In addition to the public work, the self-imposed private work done by Her Majesty is extraordinary. Every word of the Parliamentary report which is daily made to her by the leader of the House of Commons is perused by her, and not unfrequently annotated in her own hand before being filed.

Every morning the menus for all the meals are, as we know, submitted to and frequently altered by her. The COURT CIRCULAR passes through her hands, and is rigidly criticised for errors. Nor must the large private correspondence I have dwelt on be forgotten.

It may be imagined that a woman of such entirely active habits of mind and body would never be able to forgive indolence in those about her. A really idle or a merely superficial, fussy person would not be tolerated for one moment by the Queen.

It is too much the fashion in these Radical days to blame the Queen for her life of privacy, and to insinuate that one who draws such a large income from the people should be more seen of them. I wonder how many of these grumblers ever consider how long and how laborious the Queen's life has been, and how even now, at an age when most women

lie abed, or sit with idle, folded hands and fading sensibili-
ties by the fire-side, the Queen is still working early and
late for the welfare of her vast Empire and the good of
her millions of subjects.

That Her Majesty avoids the glare and glitter of mere
State ceremonial is scarcely wonderful, but beneath the
shady trees of her peaceful country retreats she is taking
no well-earned repose ; she lives in no slothful existence as the malcontents would imply. She is carrying
out to the end the precepts of the beginning, and is still
doing as she has always done, giving the best of her brain
and her heart to her country and her people. Surely she is
entitled to such rest as she can find. After all this it may
well be asked : " Does the Queen ever relax, and how ? "
Yes ; she finds in needlework and in being read to, rest for
mind and body. The study of literature and art in the
library and print room, and in the box of books from
Mudie's, are the favourite forms of idleness (?) with the
Queen. Only in knitting was Her Majesty ever awkward, and
she acknowledges herself, with a hearty laugh, the justice of
a remark made by an old peasant woman, who, unaware of
the Queen's personality, picked up a scrap of knitting that
Her Majesty had done, and curtly observed that she pitied
her " gude mon " if he got no better-made stockings than
that.

THE EAST TERRACE AT WINDSOR, SHOWING THE QUEEN'S PRIVATE APARTMENTS.

CHAPTER XXVII

THE QUEEN'S GARDENS

THE Queen's gardens at Windsor and Frogmore are adequate appendages to so regal a residence. On every side of the Castle they stretch, and each garden is different from the other, so that the passage through them is one of infinite variety. Seeing them it is easy to understand that Her Majesty's morning drives in her little basket-carriage among her grounds can never pall or grow monotonous.

History pays the first tribute to the richness of the soil about Windsor and the salubrity of its climate by showing that from the twelfth century down to Elizabeth's time, the Royal gardens were mainly vineyards, and the wine for the King's consumption was always made there. It was Elizabeth who made the first of the Terraces, the famous North Walk, which with its bastions and embrasures still overhangs the Slopes. The Virgin Queen used to stand there, and with a cross-bow shoot at the deer driven past her in the park. She also made a pleasant garden near the North Terrace, full of "meanders and labyrinths." Queen Anne afterwards remodelled this garden to commemorate Blenheim, but our Queen did the best of all with it; for she gave the plot of land some years ago to the people of the " Royal Borough " for a recreation ground.

The South Terrace is quite differently arranged. It lies between the Castle and the stables, and runs beneath the windows of Princess Henry of Battenberg's suite and of the Queen's private Audience Chamber. It is remarkable for the splendid plantation of flowering trees which the Queen has placed there. All the spring and summer through it is sweet and gay with lilacs—of which Her Majesty is very fond—may trees, laburnums, almond trees, flowering currants, and a hundred others.

Near the Slopes is the beautiful Rock Garden, planted with every kind of Alpine flower and grass. It leads to Queen Adelaide's Cottage, a charming retreat, before which stands a beech tree, called " Luther's Beech." A slab indicates that this tree was raised from the beech tree near Altenstein, beneath which Martin Luther was arrested. William IV., when Duke of Clarence, brought the little sapling to England, and planted it in Bushey Park. At Queen Adelaide's request, Prince Albert moved it to Windsor in 1850.

All large gardens have a " Fairy Dell," and that at Windsor is near Herne's Oak. More interesting, however, is the " Jubilee Walk," so called from the fact that it is bordered by goodly specimens of the evergreen oak, which were planted by the Queen and every member of the Royal Family then in England, on the very day that saw the completion of the fiftieth year of her reign. Evergreen oaks are a great feature of the Queen's gardens, and there are many magnificent ones both at Frogmore and Windsor.

The glory of Windsor is undoubtedly the East Garden, which, as it lies sunk within the embraces of the splendid raised East Terrace and the Castle, with the Victoria and Prince of Wales's Tower at either corner, and *loggias* and double staircases sweeping across the building, is the most exquisite garden outside Italy that can be imagined. The garden, which is over three acres in extent, was Charles II.'s bowling green, but Sir Jeffery Wyatville designed its present use.

It was, however, owing to the Queen's perfect taste in desiring that the flat surface of the garden should be broken up by judicious plantings of handsome shrubs, and by the delicate introduction of some very fine statuary, that the aspects of this world-famous inclosure is so charming to the eye. Two distinct plantings of flowers take place in this garden every year, and the show of tulips in the spring is particularly fine. But here, as elsewhere, no carpet bedding is allowed by the Queen, who, indeed, is too fond of Nature's children to appreciate an aspect made up of tiresome and monotonous geometrical patterns.

When the Queen is at Windsor and the weather is fine, the Guard's Band plays on the East Terrace on Sunday afternoon, and townsfolk and Royalties take their afternoon stroll in common. The East Garden was ever a favourite strolling ground with the Queen, and even now her chair passes among the statues and flower-beds, all set in fresh turf, on most days she is at the Castle.

These lovely gardens are, however, purely ornamental, and, like the pretty little inclosure at the foot of the great Round Tower, are made to be looked at only. To see the fount from which the exquisite flowers, quaint palms, rare fruits, and useful vegetables spring, that go to the Castle at least once a day, the Home Park must be traversed, Frogmore House, the Dairy, and Home Farm passed, before the high brick walls and fine gates that guard the celebrated Frogmore Gardens are attained.

Within the gates, to right and left, are two little cottages completely overgrown with Virginia creeper. One is the lodge house, and, needless to say, an old servant of the Queen's dwells therein. The other is a storehouse for apples, of which enormous quantities are grown at Frogmore. The arrangements for keeping the fruit dry and sweet are most excellent, a double-thatched roof being a great factor in the building. Leading straight from the gates is a splendid walk, with brilliant turf borders on either side. It is eleven hundred and thirty-two feet long and twenty feet wide. To the right is a magnificent line of fourteen vineries, broken only in the centre by the picturesque house of Mr. Owen Thomas, the head-gardener. On the left is a grand vista of well-filled flower beds, and a charming bell-shaped trellis, covered with roses, and also a thick, high hedge of tea roses, flowers of which Her Majesty is extremely fond. Beyond this fragrant barrier is an area of thirty-one acres, all inclosed in double lines of walls, against which are trained *en cordon*, or in the fan, pyramid, or standard style, every species of wall and stone fruit.

This splendid garden was first made in the Frogmore fields, by order of Act of Parliament, for the Queen's use early in her reign. Since then an apple orchard of four acres and twenty acres of ordinary vegetable garden have been added.

The finest sight at Frogmore is undoubtedly the conservatories and glass-houses. They are practically without number, as additions are frequently made, and they form a veritable township. The loftiest among them is the Palm House, a really fine structure containing a most valuable collection of palms, ferns, and foliage plants. Next in size is the Conservatory, where are grown every year thousands of splendid camellias, gardenias, and azalea blooms. The camellias in particular are enormous plants.

The Queen's favourite houses are those devoted to the more delicate kind of roses. These she is very fond of visiting. An interminable quantity of glass is also given up to the cultivation of flowers and foliage of every kind. It is noticeable that Her Majesty has never yielded to the fashionable craze for orchids, and only a small house is given up to the cultivation of a few ordinary kinds at Frogmore. Two houses are, however, filled with the peculiar "carnivorous" plants, which are as uncanny as they are curious, and which emit a most disagreeable odour.

The sight in these most wonderful Royal Gardens is the Pineries. There are eight pits of a total length of four hundred feet. On a hot morning when the pits are opened and each ripening pine sits like a crowned queen on her splendid throne of huge sword-edged grey-green leaves, the sight is most imposing, while the perfume can be scented half-way across the gardens. Pines for the Queen's table are grown of about eight pounds' weight, and are served to her all the year round.

Her Majesty has a fancy only to eat strawberries grown on the Frogmore estate, and wherever she may be, at home or abroad, strawberries are sent to her every day.

There being over two miles of wall at Frogmore it is easily understood that the quantity of outdoor fruit grown is immense. Two hundred and fifty varieties of pears alone are cultivated, and the same variety of apples. When fruit is grown under glass, as it ripens, each piece is carefully inclosed in a bag of white tissue paper to prevent wasps or flies from touching it.

And yet this immense garden—which is divided into eight portions, each under a foreman, who is again responsible to Mr. Owen Thomas—is scarcely large enough to supply the Royal Household, and very often there are not enough potatoes produced by the twelve acres devoted to their growth to serve the Royal residences all the year round, and others have to be bought.

Besides the outdoor asparagus beds, which are in length two thousand two hundred and twenty yards, a great deal of this delicious vegetable is grown under glass; there are also five miles of peas. Of the fruit consumed in the Royal Household the return of one year gives a fair idea.

1,673 dozens of dessert apples,

1,500 dozens and 20 pecks of pears,

1,250lbs. of cherries,

5,150lbs. of grapes,

(to which the famous old vines at Cumberland Lodge and Hampton Court contribute)

520 dozen peaches,

239 pineapples,

400 melons,

2,700lbs. of strawberries,

2,000lbs. of currants,

1,900lbs. of gooseberries,

220 dozen nectarines,

besides quantities of plums, cooking fruit, damsons, and other things. Vegetables are, of course, in like proportion, so it is easy to understand that the hundred and thirty men employed are not idle.

The Queen and all the Royal Family are great consumers of fruit and vegetables, and believe in their wholesome properties. As with the superfluous farm produce, all the garden produce that is not required at the Castles, is given away among certain people on the Royal estate.

Her Majesty is very well informed on the subject of horticulture, and is, when at Windsor, a frequent visitor to her gardens.

In Mr. Thomas' house, there is a charming room kept sacred to the Queen's use. It is at one end of the building and is entered direct from the wide main walk by a large French window which opens on to two shallow stone steps.

The wall-paper is blue with rings of gold on it. The furniture of oak with cane seats is very simple, a table fills the centre of the room, and a stuffed cockatoo gives a touch of colour. Here, facing a stone-circled fountain and pond, where some goldfish sport and a sweet-smelling Cape waterweed flourishes, Her Majesty will sit and watch her grandchildren riding small bicycles up and down the broad path and swimming boats on the pond.

The vast daily orders of fruit, flowers, and vegetables required for the Castle consumption are received by Mr. Thomas from the various departments every morning at a small wooden office which rather disfigures the beautiful old covered court just outside the door of the great kitchen. The Clerk of the Kitchen, the *chef*, and the Table Deckers whose business it is to arrange Her Majesty's board, all state to him what they want. Certain other servants are deputed to change the great plants and palms that stand in the Grand Corridor, while an entirely separate order is given for flowers wherewith to decorate Her Majesty's private apartments. Sometimes, by the Queen's special wishes, flowers are sought for among the woods and hedgerows. In the spring particularly, the Queen likes to see wild flowers in her rooms, and for days at a time bluebells and primroses will replace the rare roses and lilies that are grown at the cost of so much toil and money.

Much as the Queen loves the great gardens that give so freely of their fruit and flowers to her, the inclosed and carefully kept retreat that lies round Frogmore House is dearer to her than all. It was at Frogmore that so many happy days were passed in her early married life; it was at Frogmore that her mother, the Duchess of Kent, died and is buried; it is at Frogmore that the remains of Prince Albert are entombed; and it is at Frogmore, within a stone's throw of the pretty Tea House, where in summer she and her grandchildren breakfast, that one day she will herself lie in the peace that passes all understanding.

Frogmore House itself is, in these later days, a dull and desolate place. It is white and square and two storeys high. It is flanked by two low wings. Eight windows and a porticoed front door break the ground-floor line. A broad sweep of gravel lies before the house and encircles a great oval bed of splendid rhododendrons, the whole being secured to privacy within fine railings and gates painted black and lightly touched with gold. The evergreens and trees that border the drive are most luxuriant and seem to flourish apace in the rather damp atmosphere which rises from a small lake at the back of the house.

A set of horse-steps on the right of the front door gives a hint of many a cheery riding party in the long ago. Close by them is cut through the shrubbery the little path that leads straight to the Tea House. This is a little Bungalow of wood and "splatter work," surrounded by a small verandah, and having a conical roof of fancy red tiles. A roofed, open passage leads to a smaller building where is the little kitchen, in which tea is made and where the breakfast dishes sent every morning from the Castle in a pair-horse *fourgon* are warmed.

A polished grey granite fountain supplies the necessary water, and cream, milk, and butter are brought fresh from the Dairy opposite, which is kept and managed by two excellent Scotch women named Stoddart. The interior of the Tea House is furnished in oak. A very pretty paper with a flower-covered trellis-work pattern is on the walls, the ceiling being decorated with airy clouds and having a flying swallow painted in the centre.

The Queen sometimes takes her breakfast, which is here served entirely on silver, in the house, sometimes beneath the shade of two enormous evergreen oaks that grow before it, while two pipers play merry Scotch tunes among the trees. Tables are set on the grass, and there, with her pet dogs and her youngest grandchildren playing about her, Her Majesty dictates the ruling of her Great Empire.

A little way behind the Tea House, and hidden by the closely-grown trees, is a light iron fence. This incloses that retired spot which, in days to come, will be regarded as the cemetery of the Royal Family.

It is very beautiful and intensely peaceful, and it is easy to understand the Queen's affection for it, and to appreciate her reasons for visiting it almost every day when she is at Windsor.

There are two splendid Mausoleums here. Of the two, that which forms the tomb of the Duchess of Kent, is the more picturesque. It is shaped rather like an Indian temple, having a cupola roof supported on sixteen granite columns, and being surrounded by a terraced walk. A statue of the late Duchess stands within a niche and a bust of the Queen's half-sister is in a glass case. The building, which is of Portland stone, is approached by a beautiful little bridge swinging across the lake and half hidden by a number of splendid weeping willows. The double flight of steps leading from the bridge to the heavy oak doors is also very picturesque.

The Albert Mausoleum is larger and more imposing. It is in the shape of a cross, and the fine flight of granite steps is guarded by two imposing bronze figures of angels, one with a trumpet and the other bearing a sword. Facing the door, under a fresco of Christ breaking out of the Tomb, is the small altar. The other principal frescoes are the Cruci-fixion and the Adoration. There are many statues, among them being the figures of David, Solomon, Isaiah, and Daniel. The eight windows, in the blue-and-gold cupola, light up the white marble pillars, the golden walls, the inlaid floor, the handsome frescoes, the brilliant stained-glass, and the four bronze and gold oil lamps given by the Prince of Wales.

A very touching group is that of Princess Alice, the late Grand Duchess of Hesse, lying as though asleep on a bed, with the little child she lost her own life in trying to save, clasped in the hollow of her arm. Above her memorial hangs a picture of the Virgin and Child with St. Joseph and the Shepherds and Merchants doing homage to Our Saviour.

In the centre is Prince Albert's tomb, on which lies the imposing figure that Baron Marochetti carved in the likeness of the dead Prince. Yet most impressive of all, and a sight that brings tears to even the most hardened eyes, is the empty place by the Prince's side. It is nothing but a cold marble slab, but it cries aloud of a tender marriage, an undying affection, and a faithful, prayerful desire for a re-union in God's good time. When the day of England's sorrow dawns, the Queen will be carried here, and laid in the place where she now so often goes to pray on Sunday.

Farther away among the trees, most of which have been planted in loving remembrance by different members of the Royal Family, is the principal entrance to the sacred inclosure. It is of a lofty, classical design, having a canopy supported on pillars of granite. A big bell hangs above it.

This veritable Garden of Sleep is much beloved by Her Majesty, and is, by her orders, held sacred from all prying eyes.

THE END.